# THE EMERGENCE OF A UAW LOCAL, 1936-1939

PETER FRIEDLANDER

# The Emergence of a
# UAW Local
## 1936-1939
## A Study in Class and Culture

University of Pittsburgh Press

**Library of Congress Cataloging in Publication Data**

Friedlander, Peter, birth date
  The emergence of a UAW local, 1936–1939.
  Includes index.
  1. International Union, United Automobile Workers
of America–(CIO)–History. 2. Trade-unions–
Automobile industry workers–United States–Case
studies. I. Title.
HD6515.A8F74      331.88'12'920973      74-26020
ISBN 0-8229-3295-4

*To Edmund Kord*

# Contents

# Contents

# Acknowledgments

SPECIAL THANKS are due to David Montgomery, whose active help and encouragement were instrumental in bringing this book into existence; to Emmanuel Chill, whose example of scholarly integrity and intellectual rigor encouraged me to take the path that I did; to Bryan Palmer and Sidney Fine for their critical reading of the manuscript; and to Roberta McBride, Warner Pflug, and the staff of the Archives of Labor History and Urban Affairs at Wayne State University.

# Theory, Method, and Oral History

THIS ACCOUNT of the emergence of Local 229 of the United Automobile Workers is based on a lengthy and detailed collaboration with Edmund Kord, the president of the local during most of its first eighteen years. Because there is little documentary evidence bearing directly on the history of this local,[1] I have had to rely almost entirely on Kord's memory. For this reason I think I owe the reader an explanation of the nature and extent of these discussions and communications with Kord, so that the limitations of this study will be clear.

In December 1972 Kord and I spent eight days together on the east side of Detroit. At that time I took notes of our discussions, and Kord showed me the plant and the surrounding neighborhood in Hamtramck, pointed out the important bars, and described such details as the configuration of workers in front of the gate during strikes. I wrote a draft based on this material and on Tonat's dissertation. I sent this to Kord, along with a set of questions, for comments and criticism. On the basis of his response to these I constructed a further set of questions and sent them to him. Later, in late June of 1973, we spent a week together. This time I recorded our conversations on about eight hours of tapes. These were then transcribed and reordered in a rough narrative sequence and in this form became the basis for the major series of communications: an extensive correspondence occupying seventy-five pages. A draft of the first three chapters was then drawn up and submitted to Kord for comments and corrections. Following this we met for a week in January 1974 and two days in March 1974. Again the conversations were recorded. Finally, to fill some gaps that became apparent in the course of drawing up the final draft, Kord and I had six recorded telephone conversations totaling about four hours. What follows, therefore, is the outcome of a lengthy collaboration extending from December 1972 to March 1974.

The extent of Kord's knowlege of events in the plant varied in relation to the location of those events. Kord, who was a grinder in the torch-welding department, had an intimate knowledge of his own department and a substantial, but less intimate knowledge of the adjacent press departments, based on direct contact and close observation. His knowledge of the front of the shop—front-welding and departments 16 and 18—was gained mainly through discussions at the time with the activists and leaders in that part of the shop, although he possesses a good deal of direct knowledge even there. However, Kord's knowledge of both the toolroom and the inspection department in the early period of the union's history, with which the first chapters of this book are concerned, is limited not only by their physical distance from his own department, but also by the resistance to unionization exhibited by these two departments.

Nevertheless, because of the nature of the questions that I sought to answer in this study, the limitations imposed by the character of the evidence have little significance: not only is the necessary information unavailable except in the form of the memories of participants; it emerges only through a critical dialogue.[2] Therefore I did not simply ask questions of Kord or solicit his reminiscences. On the contrary, I sought to bring to bear on Kord's experience a number of theoretical and historical conceptions that I thought critical to an understanding of the CIO—conceptions that I found myself forced to alter as my increasingly concrete information obstinately refused to fall into some of my prefabricated categories.

Even if, for example, a certain amount of "hard" evidence were available, say in the form of census data for the plant, it would be of almost no use. The census would only distinguish between foreign-born and native-born of foreign or mixed parentage. Yet among the latter, it turns out, there were at least three distinct groups of young, unskilled second-generation Polish workers: (1) those who were helpers in front-welding and who expected to be promoted to welders (the most highly skilled production work in the plant), (2) those unskilled press operators who were in their middle twenties, who had left their parental homes, and who were married or planning to get married, and (3) those who were just out of high school (or who had dropped out) and who were members of neighborhood gangs and barroom cliques. Obviously, this kind of information cannot be gleaned from available documentary evidence.

The same problems emerge in regard to other major questions. What was the subjective, psychological content of relationships to authority, and how did this change in the course of the organizing effort? Who were the leaders: what was the inner structure of leadership, conceived of as a social formation, and how did it emerge from the matrix of social relations in the plant? What was the role of leadership, and to what extent did the leaders act or seem to act independently of their followers? How did the various groups of workers conceive of their struggle for power, and what impact did that struggle have on their personal lives and social outlooks? Until recently, the major current in labor historiography has been frankly institutional in orientation, yet the emergence of institutions is only an aspect of a more complex social process. What are the sources of institutionalization, and what is its relationship to the broader social process out of which institutions emerge?

# 1

At the heart of this small-scale study lies the necessity of grasping history as process, and, in particular, of grasping bourgeois history as the emergence, unfolding, and contradiction of specific characteristic structures. Max Weber was perhaps the first to formalize a whole cluster of key concepts, seeking to grasp the essential character of the bourgeois epoch through an examination of the significance and consequences of rationality and individualism. These concepts he elaborated in contrast to the traditionalism and the communalism of prebourgeois societies. For our purposes a critique of Weber is not suggested. On the other hand, these basic concepts, in whatever specific post-Weberian form they may take, are of singular importance in dealing with the CIO; for the presence in the industrial labor force of Eastern Orthodox Ukrainian peasants as well as Polish Catholic peasants, Slovak Lutherans as well as revolutionary nationalist Croatians, Scottish as well as Yankee tool-and-die makers, Appalachian migrants as well as migrants from the northern farm country, and acculturated urban-born blacks as well as blacks from the Delta region, demands the deployment of some kind of conceptual scheme which at the very least takes Weber as its point of departure.[3] In writing the labor history of the 1930s one is essentially dealing with the consequences of the breakdown of the *ancien régime* in eastern, southern, and southeastern Europe under the impact of the expansion of transport and the world market, and with the massive *social transformation* (one of whose dimensions is emigration) as well as geographical mobility of the peasant and artisan masses. Much of labor history thus unfolds within the ambit of the transition to capitalism, not of a particular society (say Galicia), but rather, of cultures, villages, and families.[4]

Therefore, the historic emergence of specific structures of personality and culture out of the collapse and/or transformation of a complex and variegated collection of prebourgeois cultures seems to be the crux of the problem of labor history in the thirties. Strikingly strong correlations, for example, are found between specific cultural subgroups and specific modes of practice and ideology in relation to unionism. This is the central theme of this study of Local 229. Yet labor historiography, which has tended to assume the presence of a modern, individuated, rational worker, has usually viewed the process of unionization in narrowly rational, institutional, and goal-oriented terms. The problem of culture and praxis is passed over in silence. Sidney Fine, whose books on the UAW are certainly the outstanding achievements of the institutional approach to labor history, touches only tangentially on this central problem.[5] Writing of the situation in Detroit in the 1933 to 1935 period when the AFL was attempting to organize federal unions in the auto industry, he notes that, in addition to the objective factors impeding unionization, such as seasonality and high unemployment, "the presence of a considerable number of Negroes and foreign-born in the automobile plants, particularly in the Detroit area, also posed a problem for the A.F. of L."[6] In regard to the blacks, Fine's assumptions of pragmatism emerge when he points to the racial discrimination practiced by some AFL affiliates, the racial antagonism of white workers toward blacks, Negro support for the anti-union Ford Motor Company which employed more Negroes than any other firm, and the higher rate of unemployment among blacks. These factors "deterred the Negroes from responding to union entreaties." As for the foreign-born, no explanation is given for their reluctance to join unions in this period (although Fine notes that the AFL was "reluctant to use special organizers who could appeal to the immigrant nationality groups in the industry").[7] Again, in describing the situation the UAW faced in the closing weeks of 1936, Fine states that "the majority of the automobile workers were not necessarily opposed to the UAW so much as they were waiting to see what its fate would be in a struggle with the giant employers in the industry."[8] Fine, in accounting for this situation, states that "it is difficult for a new union to organize a majority of the workers within its jurisdiction until it proves its ability to secure recognition and tangible gains for its members."[9]

The problem with this approach is not that it is wrong: such prag-matic considerations as Fine adduces were obviously real, and whatever the cultural background of the workers involved, they would have had to come to grips with these objective problems. However, the assump-tion that the workers in the plants, regardless of their historical and cultural backgrounds, exhibited a similar pattern of attitudes and be-havior that was (in Weber's terms) individualistic, rational, and goal-oriented, occludes a broad range of some of the most interesting—and important—problems of historical analysis.

Much of labor historiography (and this is true of "Marxist" accounts as well) functions on the basis of a network of unreflective conceptions or presuppositions about the nature of the individual and of the cultural matrix in which he lives. Historical formations, such as unions or political parties, are seen to be the consequences of the collective will of some section of society; for all practical purposes, moreover, that section is conceived of as an individual, and the problem is then to explain the institutional formation as the outcome of a rational process within the consciousness of this *quasi* individual. In essence, a historical formation is reduced to being the utilitarian consequence of willful behavior on the part of a rational individual. At each juncture where a gap is seen to exist between the abstractions of the political economy of work, and the concrete social reality of individual, peer group, gang, clique, family, and neighborhood—of character and culture—there appear *ad hoc* psychological notions invested with an astonishingly ubiquitous explanatory power. Such notions ignore one of the basic problems of historical thought: the nature of the relationships among these many layers of social reality. And, in regard to historical theory itself, how does one deal with the problem these relationships pose? The positivist attitude breaks down when, instead of assuming the reasonableness of the goal of unionization, one begins to scrutinize behavior itself, analyzing not only the process by which the goal is realized, but also the complex structure of cultures and relationships that develop and interact. The question then becomes not merely whether or not workers are pro-union, as if the task of the historian is to carry out an unofficial National Labor Relations Board election, but rather, what are the historical character, the specific structure, the cultural and characterological correlates, and the pattern of interaction within the diverse elements that make up the working class, as well as between these and other groups and structures in society?

By analyzing and criticizing the role of the presuppositions of possessive individualism in providing the cognitive infrastructure of labor historiography, the possibility is opened up of an analysis and interpretation of cultures in the self-formative process that has become known as "the making of the working class." But if the concept of the individual as the seat of activity is rendered historically specific and pushed to the periphery of our concerns except in those cases in which the social and historical structure of such individualism is actually present, then what is the source of activity? If history is process, what form does praxis take? Who (or what), historically speaking, actually acts?

In grappling with this problem I was concerned, in my investigations, with perceiving such historical subjects as the loci of praxis. At the outset, the work of Paul Kleppner provided a direction in the distinction he used to describe late-nineteenth-century politics, a distinction drawn from Weber between ritualistic (Catholic peasant) and pietistic (Protestant individualistic) cultures.[10] As far as ritualists were concerned, the Polish Catholic peasant immigrants in Local 229 seemed to fit

Kleppner's category. However, difficulties emerged with regard to the "pietistic" category, because the workers who were candidates for membership in this category were drawn from a variety of backgrounds, mostly Slavic. In the attempt to overcome the empirical difficulties inherent in this simplistic approach borrowed from Kleppner, I was compelled to arrive at a more general formulation of a concept of the source of praxis. Increasingly, I began to notice that I was informally grouping individuals together not in terms of their background, religion, or ethnicity (as Kleppner had done), but rather in terms of their *praxes*. Instead of identifying a sociological with a praxiological category, as Kleppner had done, I looked first at the actual patterns of activity that were emerging in the course of my investigations. What people were doing, rather than where (sociologically speaking) they were coming from, became my primary focus. For example, in the spring of 1937 a management policy change resulted in the hiring of a number of young Poles who, unknown to the management, were members of neighborhood gangs. In the course of the early history of the union drive, these workers seemed to form a group: they spoke, acted, lived, and thought together. Their relationships with the other workers, within the framework of the union, always preserved this group identity. When a situation emerged, they acted uniquely in response to it. They seemed to form a *social personality*. By focusing on practice rather than on sociological parameters it was possible to perceive coherent social formations whose activity and relationship to other such formations exhibited an internal unity.

This concept of social personality enjoys a certain rigor. It is general, at least insofar as it leaves the whole question of the form of being human open, thereby avoiding the pitfalls of operating on the basis of a presupposition of, for example, possessive individualism; and it permits a structural discipline indissolubly bound up with an empirical richness: only actual empirical investigation is permitted to contribute to a concept of a specific social personality. Social personality, conceived of abstractly, is not a thing, but rather a shorthand notation for a series of operations that the historian performs in order to arrive at a formulation of a historically specific social personality.

Having demoted the concept of the individual. we have *pari passu* demoted the concept of consciousness (at least in its Cartesian form) and thereby motivation (in the form of the will of the Cartesian individual). It no longer makes sense to ask what someone *wanted*, but rather, what he *did*, or what he was *doing*. And if there seems to be structure and coherence in history, then there must be structure to praxis. The formal, abstract task of history as a dialectical science *sui generis* is therefore to formulate a conception of this structure of a specific historical praxis, a praxis which originates within a social personality and in relation to which the "individual" becomes an object of study rather than a presupposition.

The concept of praxis demands concretization; it is incomplete without it. Yet, at the heart of this relationship between social personality and praxis lies a major contradiction. If praxis is concretized as a social personality then immediately we have established a certain kind of historical coherence, and a critical problem emerges, identified by Nancy S. Struever as follows:

Structuralists as students of culture seem to be very good at mapping totalities or coherences, which can be cultural eras or historical periods, and at showing how a particular system of reciprocal relationships maintains its identity—what used to be called the "spirit of the age." But the heart of the historical problem remains the transition between coherences, the explanation of radical discontinuity.[11]

Thus, in concretizing praxis as the activity of a social personality we a priori fail to deal with the problem of discontinuity.

Yet if we fail to concretize praxis, it remains dialectically incomplete as a concept, an empty abstraction. But is it necessary to explain the radical discontinuities? Isn't it inherent in the concept of praxis itself that there is no explanation? Man makes his own history, but only in relation to already existing conditions. Vulgar Marxism has taken the passive side of this formulation—the "conditions"—together with a set of presuppositions about the nature of man, and produced a causal theory of behavior. But Marx himself and others (e.g., Lukacs and the Frankfurt School) have always placed primary emphasis on the active side of this formulation.[12] At its root, then, the problem of history centers on understanding the relationship between praxis and structure.

In the sense that we have been using the concepts of praxis and social personality, Struever's problem of the "transition between coherences, the explanation of radical discontinuity," can be restated: even if we conceptualize a social personality as a dynamic process, wherein it may itself undergo a far-reaching historical development on the basis of an inherent generative power, this only forces us to regress a stage farther back. Struever's problem is, then, how do we explain the origins of this personality?

A partial solution to this problem focuses on the creation of new structures that by their nature cannot be reduced to the mere causal outcome of their antecedents. It is in the interaction of a number of social personalities not only with each other, but also with objective conditions, that leads to the production of higher-order historical structures. In the present case study, for example, the interaction of specific groups of workers in the plant in the context of the broader social and political processes of the New Deal era gave rise to the specific institutional structure of the local union. It would be a mistake to conceive of this structure as the direct outcome of the desires or even the actions of specific social personalities, or even to conceive of it as some kind of compromise solution. For what really unfolds is a process of reification. The institutional structure acquires a large degree of autonomy; if it is the consequence of the interaction of praxis and conditions, it nevertheless cannot be reduced to either, or even to both. The dialectic of the formation of a historical structure results in an object that owes its origins to a number of factors but which itself is more than the sum total of those factors. Finally, the participants themselves recognize this situation, and their ontological concern for the union, as an object *sui generis*, begins to overshadow their original concerns, concerns that at the outset were responsible for setting in motion the process that led to the formation of the union in the first place.

In a very real sense the problem Struever raises has its roots in religious, or at least metaphysical, concerns, for praxis is a modern and less "objectionable" way of referring to the problem of creation. To look for the creative, irreducible moment in history—to seek to observe the "self-formative process" of man—leads one to turn from the goal of causal explanation to the goal of meaningful description. Unlike the former, however, description promises no immediate understanding.

## 2

The foregoing briefly summarizes the theoretical intent of this study. Because of the nature of this investigation, however, the problem of methodology is intimately connected with the pursuit of these theoretical purposes. Since this work is almost entirely dependent on oral sources and on memory, questions emerge about the structure and reliability of memory and about the nature of the interview process itself—a problem that occupies the middle (and perhaps hybrid) ground between epistemology and linguistic philosophy, on the one hand, and more orthodox historiography on the other. For the problem that we face arises not so much out of the interpretation of data as in its creation. And because the interview process is above all linguistic, language itself becomes a methodological problem.

Superficially, of course, Kord and I shared the same language: everyday English. Moreover, Kord's cultural and social background is fairly close to that of my own family, so that, even if the results of this study might be called ethnographic, the environment I chose to study was familiar. Thus, in the collaboration that we undertook, I brought my own curiosity, informed and disciplined by a specific body of knowledge, a theoretical framework, and a rudimentary method of investigation. To these Kord added his own background in history and theory, the consequences of his father's Socialist culture, his mother's broad intellectual and cultural interests, his own schooling, his intellectual experience in the Socialist party, and, above all, his experience not merely as a participant but as the architect of Local 229. Because of Kord's cosmopolitan, rationalist background, we were able to establish a theoretical framework within which to discuss and interpret such cultural phenomena as the differences between Polish immigrants and their children. Such a theoretical framework is a vital necessity if a discussion is to get beyond the primitive stage of collecting anecdotes.

Yet in spite of this common ground, we initially had considerable difficulty with language and meaning; for history as a discipline has its own language, its canon of interpretation, its collection of problems occupying the forefront of contemporary inquiry. And my approach, a Hegelian Marxism greatly influenced by phenomenology, linguistic philosophy, and structuralism, at first only intensified this problem. Yet if the work of generating a theoretically meaningful account of the development of Kord's local union was to progress, a common language had to emerge out of our collaboration, one whose logic and terms of description would be clear and unambiguous to each of us, and within the framework of which our discussion could proceed with precision. While explicit discussion of theory would help to clarify the problems that I was concerned with, the actual emergence of our common language, and its verification, came only after months of "practice."[13] If at first our discussions seemed unclear and unfocused—if we had difficulty understanding each other—by the mid-point of our collaboration we had arrived at a sufficiently clear language and had eliminated a number of extraneous or irrelevant avenues of investigation, so that both question and answer seemed increasingly to be complementary moments in a more integrated historical discourse involving the two of us. The clarity of theoretical focus that developed, in fact, was an important part of the development of our common language.

It was within this framework of linguistic interaction that "data" was produced: since few facts existed, we had to create them. This is less arbitrary than it seems. A census enumerator, for example, does not merely collect data. Rather, standing behind him are not only the census bureau and its staff of statisticians, but also a cultural matrix and an administrative purpose which give a specific shape to certain perceptions of family structure, nationality, education, etc. Likewise, a newspaper account is hardly "factual"; it is a reporter's impression, which is itself the outcome of his predisposition to view people and situations in a certain way. Even the "obvious" fact that there were a certain number of paid-up members in the union at a particular time is a fact only because someone looked at the situation in a certain way and made an observation. (Even such hard observations can dissolve into a welter of complex, uncertain shadings and contradictory meanings when one begins to focus more closely on the phenomenology of social processes.) If, for example, the designer of the census was oblivious to the fact that Lutheran Slovaks lived in a different cultural, political, and social world than Catholic Slovaks, and that Bohemian Freethinkers were quite unlike both, the resulting category, Czechoslovak, is not only limited in its historical usefulness, but is misleading and mythological.

Thus, the historian who deals with artifacts is restricted to bringing his own intellectual apparatus to bear, not on the object itself (an epistemological fantasy at any rate), but on another object: the result of a previous process of abstraction. The limitations of depending on traditional sources are therefore obvious.

It is important to note that facts are man-made in this manner: they can only emerge and have meaning within a cultural (that is, linguistic) framework. In reality, therefore, a "fact" is a shorthand notation for the manifest results of a very complex cultural and linguistic process which gives rise to certain crystallizations of meaning. Going further, what is of deeper significance is not this manifest result as such, but the totality of the process that produces the "fact."[14] Thus, facts emerge within the framework of meaning that renders them intelligible and are the outcome of a complex process of thought and inquiry.

It follows that, once an observation is made, there is nothing sacred about it. Yet historians inevitably reify subjective human observation into immutable "facts," going so far as to prescribe unconsciously what kind of facts may exist in a totally a priori manner. Take a specific cluster of facts, and you have an "event." The usual events in labor history include strikes, acts of violence, meetings and pronouncements, as well as recessions, model changes, and elections. Obviously excluded are concepts of culture, personality, and social relationships. Yet facts can be had for the asking. For example, I asked Kord, How did the Polish immigrant workers respond to the foreman? His answer: When the foremen came around they would speed up their work, hastily crush out their cigarettes if they were smoking, etc. How did the second-generation workers react under the same conditions? They would finish their cigarettes, continue their work with no alteration, and complete their sentences. These are facts that do not appear in any documentary sources, yet they were produced in the same way that "hard" data is produced. Someone asked a question of reality.

These created facts are neither self-subsistent nor self-explanatory. They are the consequences of a specific theoretical concern about the nature of Catholic peasant communal life and of a hunch that a concept of social personality might emerge from such questions. Thus the problem of the interpretation of facts is bound up with the manner of their production: they arise out of a matrix of meaning, and they themselves may react back upon and alter that meaning. This is one of the definitions of dialectic. But these facts arise in the form of a crystallization of a moment in the unfolding of a specific intellectual praxis. What is important, therefore, is not the collection or even the explanation of facts, but rather the development of a historically concrete conception of praxis out of the strategy of formulating and asking the right questions in order to get crystals of meaning appropriate to the intent of the investigation. These "facts" about the first- and second-generation Poles emerged because my question elicited them. The archetypal question was always, What are people doing, what is their praxis? Rigorous description, rather than causal explanation, became the object of this investigation.

Looked at in this way [writes Clifford Geertz], the aim of anthropology is the enlargement of the universe of human discourse . . . it is an aim to which a semiotic concept of culture is particularly well adapted. As interworked systems of construable signs (what, ignoring provincial usages, I would call symbols), culture is not a power, something to which social events, behaviors, institutions, or processes can be causally attributed; it is a context, something within which they can be intelligibly—that is, thickly, described.[15]

The concept of "thick description" projects a strategy of perception that is open-ended and concrete; whose dialectic seeks, not simplification and reduction to basic concepts, but elaboration and increasing complexity. But is this a form of impressionism, a renunciation of theory as such?

Theoretical formulations hover so low over the interpretations they govern that they don't make much sense or hold much interest apart from them. This is so, not because they are not general (if they are not general, they are not theoretical), but because, stated independently of their applications, they seem either commonplace or vacant. . . . the essential task of theory building . . . is not to codify abstract regularities but to make description possible, not to generalize across cases but to generalize within them . . . Rather than beginning with a set of observations and attempting to subsume them under a governing law, such inferences begin with a set of (presumptive) signifiers and attempts to place them within an intelligible frame.[16]

The relationship of theory to description is essential. The analytic (and positivist) paradigm tends to reduce observation to basic analytical categories related by laws. Implicit in this process is a dualistic conception of the relationship between theory and observation. The descriptive side of the process either provides data which, grasped properly under the aegis of analysis, exemplifies some general law, or it defies analysis, thereby compelling the modification of the present theory or the formulation of a new one. But there is no dialectic: analytic theory either reduces the data, or the data challenges the theory.

But Geertz suggests that the goal of theory in anthropology (and as far as I am concerned, also in history) is not to reduce observation to exemplifying basic laws, but to make description "thickly" possible. This reversal of roles is related to a reversal of orientation. Instead of manipulating nature and society, the human sciences seek to understand the self-formative process of man.

The emphasis on description as something that theory helps to shape highlights the importance of language in Marxist historiography. If the role of theory is to make thick description possible, and if description is a linguistic activity, then the role of theory is to enable us to shape a language appropriate to the object to be described. Once the problem is formulated this way, an important shift of focus occurs. "But, as, in the study of culture, analysis penetrates into the very body of the object— that is *we begin with our own interpretations of what our informants are up to, or think they are up to, and then systematize those*—the line between . . . culture as a natural fact and . . . culture as a theoretical entity tends to get blurred."[17] Thus, the historical situatedness of the historian himself renders his own thought problematical. This dialectic between subject and object, always the primary concern of the Hegelian and Hegelian-Marxist, is, as Struever's article indicates, emerging as a primary concern of a large number of historians. But, except for recent history, the historian is faced with artifacts, and the distinction between these (which belong to the object) and the historian (as subject) is, on the surface at least, fairly sharp. Artifacts, after all, don't talk back. In the present work, however, this distinction is blurred. The object of study, Local 229, is available in the form of one of its architects, Edmund Kord. And, far from being a barrier, the absence of artifacts (except for a handful) was an opening, an opportunity for creating these crystallizations of meaning in a manner reflective of the concerns of this investigation. It is the character of this situation that inevitably forces the historian to reflect on his own activity when he attempts to write history.

Language was crucial: in the absence of artifacts, there remained the speaking that filled the air between Kord and me. It is here that the general idea of generative grammar (or rules of transformation), the objective of thick description, and historical theory come together.[18] If theory ought, as Geertz states, to enable us to "intelligibly, that is, thickly," describe historical processes, then the structure of this description, the rules for the formation of language, is the theory. That is, theory ought to be functionally inseparable from description. Theory is a way of structuring perceptions, not in the sense of analytic theory, which reduces perception to a category, but in the sense of rendering what is concrete meaningful without robbing it of its concreteness. And the operations that unfold in the historian's "consciousness," the way he looks at reality, the way he seeks meaning and thereby structures his perceptions, and finally, the generative grammar of the language specific to a work of history, are the theory.

Theory as such is not seen; rather, it is the logic that makes seeing possible in the form of thick description. For example, Weber's concept of the Protestant ethic does not appear as such in the description of the leadership cadres of Local 229, but the concept of the Protestant ethic, the manifold of perceptual and cognitive strategies that it opened up, lay behind and in fact generated the specific linguistic "games" that Kord and I constructed in our effort to meaningfully comprehend, or thickly describe, the leadership cadre of the local. Thus, in contrast to the static and undialectical procedure of orthodox historiography, Kord and I were continually shaping and reshaping historical concepts to fit the emerging pattern of Local 229, attacking the history of the local from various angles, seeking to elicit different groups of facts—facts about personality, about ethnic cultures, and about the structure of small groups and their relationship to the structure of the local. Consequently, we were able to investigate aspects of social life that never leave sufficient traces in documents, newspaper accounts, memoirs, and other materials. The range of this kind of investigation was obviously limited by the structure and reliability of Kord's memory.

Kord's willingness and intellectual ability to enter into this system of thought were critical to the success of this venture. However, these necessary conditions were not in themselves sufficient. The size and layout of the plant as well as the personality and role of the informant, were also key factors. Because the Detroit Parts Company was small, employing at most five hundred workers, and since it was essentially contained on the ground floor of a single large shed, a worker could see and know the whole field of activity, either directly or through close contacts in other departments. Because there were so few workers, because the union, over the years, became a closely knit community, and because its administrative structure was open-ended and broad-based, Kord was able to become acquainted with a large number of the workers. Because Kord has a broad intellectual background; because he was one of the union's chief organizers, compelled by the nature of his task to acquire a broad and detailed knowledge of the shop; and because he occupied a position of responsibility which demanded he take a close look at situations and make hard-nosed decisions, his perceptions acquired a definitiveness and rigor that are usually absent even in secondary leaders. In addition, Kord has a magnificent memory.

But how reliable is Kord's memory? This is a problem that encompasses any oral history project, and it must be dealt with forthrightly. Kruchko has observed that, in his interviews with veterans of the struggle to organize UAW Local 674 in Norwood, Ohio, "the memories of the men . . . even down to small details, were surprisingly accurate."[19] I found the same to be true of Kord. The depth and intensity of his involvement was such that even now, thirty-six years later, his remembrances are both vivid and detailed.

Nevertheless, memory does not provide us with the kind of pinpoint accuracy found in documentary evidence. Kord's margin of error in the precontract period, he estimates, is of the order of several days to two weeks. Thus, I refer to a meeting which was held during the last part of February, for example. How important such a margin of error is depends upon how well Kord could recall the dramatic sequence of events not only in terms of order, but also in terms of the tempo and dynamic of development. In this regard Kord's memory was generally clear and unambiguous, and he was quite certain of all but a handful of minor points. Nevertheless, in addition to the external verification, which was found in the few sources that relate to Local 229 and which appears in the footnotes, a system of internal checking was also used. As the broad picture began to emerge in the course of our discussions and correspondence, I in effect "cross-examined" Kord. In general, the contradictions that I found were relatively minor, more often than not based on misunderstandings. In addition, these contradictions were ironed out early in the course of our work: Kord, having become deeply involved in this endeavor, began to do his own checking. Wherever any uncertainty has remained, it is indicated.

Yet if the contents of memory are simply "facts" as discussed above, we would find ourselves in the same situation that obtains when dealing with more orthodox sources. But while the structure of memory is related to the structure of perception and the latter is itself rooted in culture, education, and experience (native American informants, for example, are extraordinarily unperceptive about Slavs), memory itself is a vast welter of impressions and feelings, as well as a more structured, rational schemata. Many impressions either were not important to Kord in 1937 or did not appear to make any sense; yet, as we brought them to the foreground their possible interconnectedness and meaning emerged. Furthermore, the elaboration of this matrix of meaning and the gradual construction of the history of the local reacted back upon the original source, Kord's memory. As a consequence, Kord's recollections became richer and more precise, and the elaboration of a number of hypotheses gave a critical focus to his effort to recall. And precisely because memory is richer than the rational narrative superstructure to which it is often reduced, the whole enterprise remained open-ended: there were numerous ways of structuring the material. What it would become depended on how we approached our work, what leads we followed, and what problems concerned us. For example, I continued to press for cultural and psychological data on as many workers as Kord could remember, especially the primary and secondary leadership. Certain Freudian and Weberian concerns led me to ask particular kinds of questions (e.g., about personal habits such as drinking). These questions themselves emerged in my own thought only over a period of many months, and the responses to them were by no means immediately intelligible. I was looking for patterns and relationships. At first, however, the material was necessarily fragmentary; then, after more such questions and answers had accumulated, the material became less fragmentary, but it was still difficult to penetrate. Only gradually did patterns emerge relating some characteristics of personality with certain aspects of the history of the local.

Two further examples help clarify the relationship between memory and theory. In the course of our first series of discussions in December 1972, Kord made a remark about "new hires" in department 19 (in the spring of 1937). The remark registered, but I let it go by. Later, as we continued to discuss the situation in the plant, "new hires" came up again. What gave the department where these employees worked its peculiar character was the fact that they were members of neighborhood gangs. Yet what I had at this point was not a concept of a social group, but rather the understanding that very likely these gang kids were in fact a group, that they had to be studied further, and that out of all this a concept might emerge. In the next series of discussions and in the seventy-five pages of letters that I sent to Kord, whenever relevant I brought up questions relating to these young workers. What did they say to the foreman under certain circumstances? What forms of recreation did they engage in? Where did they live, and under what circumstances? What were their attitudes toward the union effort at specific times? How did they react to the five-cent raise? The results of such inquiry are contained in the body of the book.

Another determination I sought out more purposefully. I was convinced that there were significant ethical or moral differences between the Appalachian migrants, the first-generation Slavs, and the wildcatters among the second generation. Twice in the course of our second series of discussions (July 1973) I raised this question. Twice Kord replied negatively. The third time, however, something clicked. Kord briefly but cogently described actual confrontations, quoted typical statements made by representative members of the three groups, and described the interrelationship of these groups within the union and their different relationships to the leadership in confrontation situations. Further, he discussed their varying attitudes toward authority, both that of the management and that of the union leaders, and their conceptions of society, of the individual, and of standards of behavior.

This example illustrates both the obstacles to and the immense potential of this kind of investigation. The process of searching, guessing, hypothesizing, and probing that the historian must undertake depends for its success on the degree to which his collaborator is willing to get involved in these questions. Often the relevance of what I asked was not obvious, and some of the more exciting questions were obscure and even ambiguous. To make sense out of some of my questions required that Kord search his memory for any evidence that might have had a bearing on the question, sort it out, and verbalize it. If these cultural differences were not clear at the time, then Kord's cognitive processes did not organize his perceptions along such lines. Such an organization of perceptions, drawn from the complex welter of memory, was precisely what I asked of Kord. And it was here that a real dialectic unfolded, in the course of which we collectively shaped both concept and perception, batting ideas and observations around, exploring their significance, and conceiving of new questions as material developed.

From the foregoing, it is obvious that, if certain problems are to be explored at all, they must be investigated through the use of oral history techniques: the usual sources that historians traditionally rely upon simply fail to throw any light on some of the most fundamental historical processes. Yet even in those areas of data collection where the census is thought to excel, oral history techniques are far more accurate than any but the most accurate hypothetical census. For example, we have already seen one of the problems with the census—its tendency to amalgamate under a single category (such as Czechoslovak) several distinct and often contradictory social groups. Beyond this, however, even if the ethnic composition of a factory were known to a high degree of precision, its relevance would remain dubious. Of what value would be the knowledge that 30 percent of the workers in a particular plant were Polish, if we knew from previous investigations that this geographical unit was far too large to be meaningful? On the other hand, the response of an informant that a single department, say metal-finishing, possessed a work force that was 90 percent Polish might be off by a few points, or even by as much as 10 or 15 percent, but it would be far closer to the truth than the census estimate, which would be unable to go any farther than specifying that 30 percent of the workers *in the plant* were Polish. When one realizes that each department possessed a very specialized ethnic structure, it becomes obvious that if one is to write the social history of the organization of a factory, one must have this information; and from the standpoint of the historian, such data, regardless of the greater margin of error of this technique, is far more useful and indeed, from a historiographical standpoint, far more accurate than the results of a hypothetical census based on plant-wide surveys.[20]

To meaningfully describe patterns of behavior or to analyze the structure of an event are objectives that often lie beyond the reach of orthodox uses of data, particularly when one's interest shifts from the various intellectual, social, and political elites to the industrial working class. In the present study, for example, a critical union action inside the plant is met with strikingly different positive responses on the part of the first- and the second-generation Poles. Such occurrences provide invaluable materials out of which to develop a sense of the interaction of the various political cultures within the plant—or they even permit one to define such cultures in the first place.

Nevertheless, in the conduct of a series of interviews it is important to maintain a critical attitude. Failure to cross-examine can lead to astonishing reversals of fact. For example, in an interview by Jack Skeels of Frank Fagan, a unionist active in the Murray Body plant during the formative years of the UAW, an entirely different story emerges from that found in my own interviews with Fagan.[21] In the Skeels version, an incident in 1933 in which Fagan organized a petition campaign among thirty welders asking for company-supplied leather armlets to protect their clothing and arms from red-hot sparks resulted in the firing of Fagan and another worker. This event, according to Fagan, "broke the back of the men." In this section of the interview, Skeels himself intervened very infrequently, resulting in long periods of unbroken reminiscences which were left to stand as they were, with no effort made at cross-examination or elicitation of detail. Unprepared for what was to follow, I reopened the question of the leather armlet incident with Fagan, mainly in order to investigate the ethnic background of the workers involved and the structure of the event. This eighteen-minute section of the interview began with a discussion of the year. Fagan thought that it was 1935. I told him that in his previous interview he had said 1933. He was unable to remember that interview, but began to fix the leather armlet incident in relation to other events, finally settling on 1935 as the most likely year. The story then unfolded in great detail; I constantly asked for more bits of information— the names of people, descriptions of the welding process and the problem it posed in terms of burning holes in the welders' shirts, etc. Then I asked Fagan to remember as many individuals as he could who were working on the same line and who got involved in the petition incident. At this point the interview makes for poor reading: long periods of silence, punctuated first by one name—about whom I asked such details as ethnic background and union experience—then by another name, the whole liberally sprinkled with remarks by Fagan that this was a long time back and was hard to remember, yet at the same time that he could visualize all of the welders involved in the incident. Nevertheless, he succeeded in remembering eight others besides himself. He described the incident itself: the misgivings of many of the workers about signing the petition, its delivery, and the response of the personnel manager to Fagan and his coworker Udata as he politely threw them out onto the street. From this point on, however, the story directly contradicts the earlier version told to Skeels. Following the firing of Fagan and Udata, some of the welders began a job action, letting the arcs of flame get too big and burning holes in the automobile bodies, as a result of which production of the entire plant was piling up in the repair shop. The foreman told all the welders to go home and to behave themselves when they returned the next day. Alex Faulkner replied (as was reported to

Fagan a few days later) that Fagan and Udata both better be at work too. Within a couple of days the company had gotten in touch with Fagan and rehired him. When Fagan returned to work, however, the other workers wanted to know where Udata was, and Fagan, after a visit to Udata's home, ascertained that Udata had gotten another job, not wanting to return to Murray Body. Only then did the tension subside.

The point of retelling this story is to illustrate some of the pitfalls of writing oral history. Memory is a treacherous thing, as more than one of my informants has remarked. The necessity for cross-examination, digging for details, and even confronting an interviewee with contradictory evidence, is critical. It is important *before* the interview to get deeply into the documentary materials relevant to an interviewee's experience, to anticipate several strategies of questioning, and to be prepared with a battery of questions that are derived from the historian's special understanding of social phenomena. It is equally necessary to be alert to the possibility that an offhand remark may contain an important clue, the consequences of which may be totally unexpected and even contrary to some basic assumptions. In general, the historian must counterpose his *intensive* approach to the *extensive* narrative that tends to be the spontaneous response of most informants. Thus, in the Skeels interviews, there are numerous junctures in which an informant reveals something of critical significance. Instead of interceding and sharpening the focus of the discussion, Skeels let these things go by. In fairness to Skeels, of course, we should remember that many of these theoretical concerns are of recent origin. Nevertheless, as the leather armlet incident indicates, there may be some question about the accuracy of interviews conducted in an expansive narrative style, rather than through intensive cross-examination.

## 3

Because of the difficulties of studying a large plant, it seems unlikely that a study of a scope similar to the present one could be carried out without the cooperation of dozens of leading activists, coordinated over several months, and involving perhaps hundreds of hours of discussions with each of them. Even so, the anonymity of the mass of the workers in a large plant makes this a difficult—perhaps impossible—enterprise. On the other hand, the documentary records of the large locals—particularly the Dodge local—are quite extensive. But by themselves these materials permit little more than the usual institutional approach to labor history.

It is important to be aware of these limitations. After all, it was the large locals that were the political power centers, and it was these same locals that became the battleground of the factional warfare of 1938–1939. Was the internal development of Local 229 essentially similar to that of Local 3 (Dodge)? Or did the position of the Dodge local as the key center of the UAW in Detroit have an important influence on its internal development? It seems impossible to arrive at any understanding of the political and organizational struggles within the leadership of the UAW without establishing a solid foundation of several studies of key locals. Nevertheless, the examination of a small local does shed a considerable amount of light on these broader questions (discussed in chapter 8).

Kord has asked that, with the exception of UAW officials, the names of all persons appearing in this study be changed, and that the identity of the company be rendered obscure. To accomplish this the product itself must necessarily remain unspecified. However, the original materials are being prepared for deposit in the Archives of Labor History and Urban Affairs at Wayne State University in Detroit, subject to whatever conditions Kord wishes to place upon their use.

In view of the foregoing, one can judge how much I owe to Kord: we have truly collaborated in this effort, and the amount of time he put in has been enormous. Whatever merit this work has, a large share of the credit is his.

# THE EMERGENCE OF A UAW LOCAL, 1936-1939

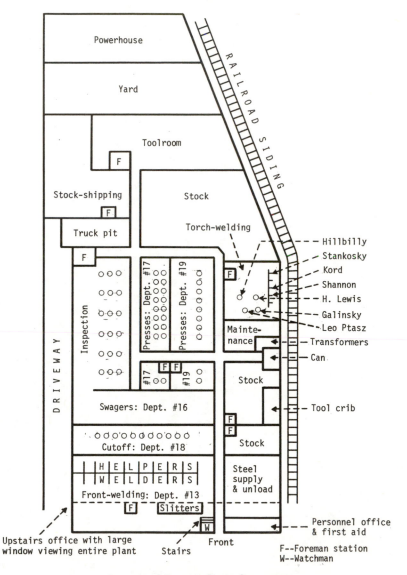

Powerhouse

Yard

Toolroom

F

Stock-shipping

F

Stock

Truck pit

Torch-welding

F

Inspection

Presses: Dept. #17

Presses: Dept. #19

Maintenance

#17

F F

#19

Swagers: Dept. #16

Cutoff: Dept. #18

H E L P E R S
W E L D E R S

Front-welding: Dept. #13

F

Slitters

W

DRIVEWAY

RAILROAD SIDING

Stock

Can

Stock

Tool crib

F
F

Stock

Steel
supply
& unload

Hillbilly
Stankosky
Kord
Shannon
H. Lewis
Galinsky
Leo Ptasz
Transformers

Personnel office
& first aid

Upstairs office with large
window viewing entire plant

Stairs       Front

F--Foreman station
W--Watchman

**Layout of Detroit Parts Company**
(based on a drawing from memory by Edmund Kord)

# CHAPTER ONE

# In the Beginning

## Background

THE MOST SALIENT FEATURE of the Detroit Parts Company was its location in one of the most important Polish communities in the United States; conversely, it was due to the automobile industry that Hamtramck became a predominantly Polish community, for with the establishment of the Dodge plant a large number of Poles swarmed into Hamtramck, increasingly displacing the earlier Irish and German inhabitants of the area.[1] The Poles who settled there, unlike those who settled the steel and coal areas of Pennsylvania, came not directly from Poland but rather from other parts of the United States, although a large number of them had originally been immigrants.[2] Because of this secondary nature of Polish settlement in Hamtramck, the old country localism was weakened, and a more general sense of Polish national identity characterized the Hamtramck community.[3] While a large number of the Poles who moved to Hamtramck were of peasant origin, perhaps 10 percent were of urban and artisan backgrounds.[4] Moreover, wide variations in historical development existed in Poland and were reflected in the social and political outlooks of the immigrants, in their family structure, and in their education and occupation. Even among the immigrants of agrarian background distinctions must be made between those who came from the backward villages of Galicia, for example, and those who came from the environs of Warsaw or Cracow or Lodz.[5] A number of Polish immigrants had already worked in factories, and some had come into contact with trade unions and socialism before coming to this country. Furthermore, although the Polish peasant who came from the more backward agricultural areas was relatively uneducated, a significant number of immigrants had acquired considerable education, either formally or in the home, where respect for education and a high degree of literacy were part of the artisan heritage.

In the United States, the social and cultural differentiation within the mass of Polish immigrants became increasingly complex. The disintegration of family ties accelerated, and a process of individualization unfolded with increasing rapidity, especially among the children of immigrants.[6] A small number of second-generation Poles became assimilated to the extent that they identified with previous groups of Catholic immigrants: the Irish and the German. They fell under the influence of Father Coughlin[7] and later appear to have become one of the bases of the Association of Catholic Trade Unionists. In addition, the character of their attachment to Catholicism was strikingly different from that of the mass of Polish workers. They went to English-speaking churches, developed an ascetic and puritanical outlook, and in this way distinguished themselves sharply from the adherents of the less rigid, more sensual Catholicism of the Slavic churches. Furthermore, whereas the mass of the second-generation Polish men were only nominally Catholic, these few assimilated Poles had a much deeper attachment to the church, although it must be added that the church functioned for them perhaps more as a cultural and social organization than as a religious one. If they were few in numbers, their cohesiveness and activism gave them a disproportionately large role to play in the UAW, where they frequently became leading but conservative trade unionists.

Within the Polish Catholic churches there was little support and much opposition to the UAW in 1936 and 1937 (later the churches would accept the union as an accomplished fact). As far as the Catholic clergy were concerned, "most of them showed open hostility to the very idea unionism and Communism."[8] Instead, the UAW had to rely on the sympathy of the lodges of sick and death benefit organizations such as the Polish National Alliance, the Polish Roman Catholic Union, and the Polonia Society of the International Workers Order. In the latter part of 1936 a Polish Trade Union Committee was established, consisting of Polish workers from shops throughout the city.[9] The importance of these community organizations cannot be overestimated, for the communal aspect of the organization of the Polish workers seems to be one of the most important characteristics of the UAW in Detroit. In contrast, the semiskilled production workers such as trimmers and metal finishers tended to supply shop-floor impulses and organizational leadership. These workers were a heterogenous mixture of native Americans, Irish and Germans, as well as second-generation Poles whose community ties were weaker and whose individuation was far more advanced than that of the first-generation immigrants. Among the Poles in the Detroit Parts Company it was this second generation that provided the early initiative, the first real base, and much of the structure of leadership.

Because the automobile industry was far more decentralized in this early period, wherever major producers located opportunities were created for independent entrepreneurs to establish themselves in the shadow of the larger corporations. Thus, the creation of the mammoth Dodge Brothers Manufacturing Company in 1914, employing at its peak twenty-seven thousand employees, inevitably attracted both workers and entrepreneurs. Stretching along the east and west borders of Hamtramck there sprang up a large number of secondary and feeder plants whose economic well-being depended on that of the major companies. Some of these specialized plants were clustered together just north of the Dodge plant on the east side of Hamtramck. The Detroit Parts Company, founded soon after the First World War by William Perkins and the Swedish brothers J. A. and Walter Bergson, was one of them.

William Perkins provided the capital (his wife's ten thousand dollars) while the Bergson brothers provided the technical ability. When the company was founded, the welding and shaping of _____ had hardly been developed. At that time a slow, crude, and expensive method was the only one available. But the discoveries of the Bergsons promised the newly founded firm success. Electrical welding, hitherto undeveloped in this area, and a method of bending and forming _____, quickly captured a large share of the _____ market for the Detroit Parts Company, while the licensing of its patent rights brought in additional income. The company was primarily dependent on the automobile industry, with a significant but smaller part of its output going into the manufacturing of furniture. Overall, the Detroit Parts Company was doing well.

Perkins himself fit the folk image of the independent entrepreneur.

He used to boast that he was a "self-made man," although it was his wife's money and the Bergsons' knowledge that had made him. Once a week he would come down from his office and tour the plant, talking to no one. He would stop occasionally, pick up a piece of work, turn it over in his hand, scrutinize it, and put it down again. In part this routine was a kind of sham: he knew much less than he pretended about production and technology. Perkins affected a gruff tone of voice, and his manner was peremptory. As an entrepreneur he was more style than substance. With respect to the deployment of his capital he proved to be suicidally conservative. After the Second World War the company was faring poorly. Technical changes, the expiration of its patents, and the changing structure of the market threatened its existence. When the union pointed out that Perkins could recoup his business by diversifying, he replied, "This is a ＿＿＿ company, and its going to stay a ＿＿＿ company!"

In his dealings with the workers Perkins, the president, and to a lesser extent J. A. Bergson, the plant manager, showed a rigidity and arrogance that would ultimately contribute to their defeat at the hands of the union. Failing to perceive the complex reality of the labor situation in the plant, these two men showed such poor judgment that they initiated policies which not only failed to stop the union, but on the contrary proved to be indispensable to its success.

Prior to the CIO drive of 1937, the Detroit Parts Company had a confrontation with militant workers, the outcome of which altered the options that would exist in 1937. In the fall of 1933 Detroit was marked by an upsurge of activity and organization among the highly skilled craftsmen in the automobile industry. Among the organizations that emerged, the Mechanics Educational Society of America (MESA) is the best known, but others, such as the Dingman's Welfare Club and the Society of Designing Engineers, also made their appearances. [10] Whether any organizational connection existed between the MESA and the activity in the Detroit Parts Company is not known. At the same time, however, a number of toolmakers and inspectors, led by a law student working in the inspection department, banded together and succeeded in negotiating a pay increase. Failing either to establish a formal organization or to sign a contract, they found themselves in a precarious position; and at its first opportunity the company fired all

but one of them. Al Schein, who was on this first negotiating committee, not only retained his employment, but was promoted to floor
inspector and given a raise in pay. (This and other pieces of evidence
would later convince the leadership of UAW Local 229 that Schein was
a spy.)

The uprooting of these early unionists and the activities of Schein
would have far-reaching effects on subsequent events. As a floor inspector, Schein was one of the few workers with the run of the shop and
could report back to the management any signs of union sentiment. In
addition, he was able to intimidate the other workers in his department
to the extent that in 1937 the union would be unable to establish even
a foothold in inspection until after the signing of the first contract.
Thus, the strategic situation that would obtain in 1937 was shaped to a
great extent by what happened in 1933: a group of militants was
removed from the back of the shop, and inspection was provided with a
strong anti-union leader.

A further consequence was even more far-reaching: new men, more a
part of the life of the Slavic community in which the plant was
embedded, would rise to leadership. They would have a new attitude
toward the mass of unskilled Slavic workers in the shop and would
shape a very different union.

The company, too, may have drawn its lessons from this experience.
Certainly, the ease with which this group of unionists was eliminated
must have encouraged Perkins and Bergson to persist in their one-sided
and peremptory approach to labor relations. They would discover to
their dismay that the strategy of union-busting must be developed from
a closer and more realistic understanding of the concrete situation; and
this situation had changed drastically by 1937.

To some extent the history of Local 229 begins, not in the production facilities of the Detroit Parts Company, but in a flat owned by one
of the foremen. Edmund Kord, whose sister occupied the flat, had been
born in this country, returned to Poland, where he grew up, and as a
young man had come back to Hamtramck in 1934. On his father's side
there is a family memory of a German element (although by the
twentieth century it had become thoroughly Polonized) within which
had unfolded a conflict between Protestantism and Catholicism. Although the Catholic side—Kord's great-grandmother or her mother—

won out upon the death of her husband, Kord's father, a cooper living in the vicinity of Warsaw, was both a Socialist and an anticlerical. These feelings were to a great extent shared by Kord's mother, who as a servant girl in a middle-class family in Warsaw had acquired an education and associated with theater people, developing numerous intellectual interests and a sense of independence. In contrast with the extended family structure characteristic of the peasant immigrants in Hamtramck, Kord's family was individuated, fragmented, dispersed, and nuclear. Throughout his life Kord had a strong intellectual drive. At first denied admission to the Gymnasium in Warsaw, he fought his case through the bureaucracy and after a year won entrance. Returning to Detroit in 1934, Kord, like hundreds of thousands of other American workers, desperately sought work in the capital of the crippled automobile industry. Hunger and insecurity were his constant companions.

In 1935 Kord, in need of a job, was staying at his sister's. Through her he met Bob Toller, a foreman at the Detroit Parts Company, who recommended Kord for a job at the plant. The plant manager, J. A. Bergson, was hesitant. "I'd like to give you a job," he said, "but you have a good education, and our experience has been that people with a good education cause trouble." Most likely, Kord thinks, Bergson was referring to the law student of 1933. Kord managed—sincerely—to convince him he meant no trouble. ("All I wanted was a job," Kord recalls, "I never intended any trouble . . .") In fact, Kord was aiming at a career in teaching, not unionism. Nevertheless, he would become the preeminent and perhaps indispensable organizer of UAW Local 229.

When Kord came to work in 1935, the grayness and drabness of the plant, the noise and the dirt, and the autocratic and capricious regimen of industrial discipline seemed to be reflected in the workers themselves. Subordinated to machines and to a system of production, they seemed stripped of their individuality. Without bonds of friendship or feelings of sympathy they passed their working hours in isolation and loneliness. To Kord they looked like "a gray mass evidencing no hope, no aspirations, no capabilities, no talents. . . . People kept to themselves. . . . They did their work and not much else." For the first year and a half during which Kord worked at the plant this depressing existence continued. As far as organization was concerned, the word *union* was never mentioned in the shop; and Detroit itself was quiet.

Toward the end of 1936, however, this picture had begun to change. The Roosevelt landslide had altered the political climate. The election, said a CIO leader in Detroit, [was] "a mandate to organize."[11] Even more significant than its impact, though, the election landslide was a result of the unprecedented political awakening of the masses of new immigrants—the Poles, Slovaks, Croatians, Lithuanians, Ukrainians, Slovenians, and Italians. In industrial cities with large immigrant populations such as Pittsburgh, Cleveland-Youngstown, Chicago-Gary, Buffalo, and Detroit, the rush to the polls was of flood proportions: voter turnout in these areas in 1936 was nearly twice that of 1932. On the other hand, voter turnout increased only marginally in such labor strongholds as Minneapolis and Toledo, where the population was predominantly of native American or north European background.[12] The election of Roosevelt was therefore not the cause of this immigrant upheaval, but it helped to focus and express it. And, more than ever before, the governing party rested on a coalition which included these newly awakened immigrants and their children, labor, and a strong current of prolabor liberalism. Hamtramck itself would become a major stronghold of the New Deal Democratic Party, giving over 90 percent of its votes to FDR in subsequent elections.[13]

The Slavic workers in the Detroit Parts Company were a part of this upsurge. The New Deal was very popular among them, and although Kord has no way of knowing for sure, he suspects that large numbers of these workers voted for the first time in 1936. "There was a visible amount of enthusiasm; and there was a feeling of hope."

In October the UAW had already gained a victory over the question of seniority in the Dodge plant, but the floodgates seemed to open after the November election. In South Bend, Indiana, the workers at the Bendix plant staged a sit-down on November 17, 1936. On the twenty-seventh of that month the workers at Midland Steel sat down. The resulting shortage of steel frames caused the layoff of at least fifty-three thousand workers at the Plymouth, Dodge, Chrysler, Lincoln-Zephyr, and Briggs plants. On December 4 the UAW won a significant victory over Midland Steel. Also during this month there were several sit-downs in Detroit at National Automotive Fibres, Bohn Aluminum, Alcoa, and Kelsey-Hayes. The sit-downs crippled production at the Rouge plant, owing to a shortage of brake shoes and drums. Such strikes were like " 'a brilliant meteor flaming across the dark sky,' " bringing the union a good deal of publicity, and providing it with the "aura of victory." [14] They were discussed by the workers at the Detroit Parts Company. Midland Steel was only half a mile from the plant, and the strike "hit home pretty hard. Everybody was talking about it." To some of the workers in the plant the organization of the automobile industry now seemed to be a distinct, if still somewhat remote possibility.

### First Efforts and the Emergence of Cadre

Several months after Kord had begun work in department 17, he was transferred to torch-welding, where he became a grinder. Toller, the foreman in this department, had been instrumental in effecting this move. It was a token of friendship on his part, for torch was a better department to work in. After Kord had been transferred, he became acquainted with Shannon, a grinder who worked beside him. Their friendship was relatively superficial, however, and was thus characteristic of the relationships among the workers at this time. Their contact did not extend beyond the plant.

There was something about Shannon that even then made him stand out in a situation where all individuality was crushed. A young Irish migrant from the coal fields of Punxsutawney, Pennsylvania, he was an outgoing, amiable, and courageous person. His active experience with the United Mine Workers had been slight, but he had a strong belief in the cause of trade unionism. As far as Kord knows, he was the only worker in the plant with such a background. Although Shannon was nominally a Catholic, he rarely if ever went to church, was divorced, and could be boisterously iconoclastic at times. He spent a lot of time in bars, went on frequent benders, and enjoyed the companionship of what Kord could only describe as a series of "floozies." He was mischievous, something of a rogue, and would, in the course of the union struggle, become immensely popular with the rest of the workers.

He emerged at the outset as one of the union activists and quickly became one of the four major leaders in the shop.

When in December 1936 Kord decided to organize a union in the shop, he turned first to Shannon. Even so, it was not clear to Kord that Shannon would go along with the idea. But they had already discussed the strikes that were breaking out, and they "must have communicated [their] sympathies to each other. When [Kord] approached him finally it was no doubt in terms of looking up the UAW. Only the UAW was identified as the 'union.' And in some ways the CIO [and John L. Lewis] overshadowed the UAW." Kord and Shannon agreed to contact people on the job.

In the course of these discussions Shannon began referring to Kord, who had enrolled in the evening division of Wayne University earlier that year, as the "professor." Almost immediately the name caught on among the others in the department. (There were a number of similar cases around Detroit of highly educated workers being called by this name.)

The first phase of activity occurred early in January 1937. The Flint sit-down strike was under way and to some extent influenced their expectations. Although at this early stage they did not dare to move out of their own department, they thought that if the UAW were contacted it would start a drive in the whole shop. ("Little did we know that there was so much similar activity in the whole city that there was not enough UAW to go around. It turned out that we would have to . . . do it ourselves with a minimum of help from the UAW.") Kord suggested that they immediately contact the UAW. Shannon agreed, but thought that three of them should go. Leo Ptasz, a second-generation Polish welder, was enlisted after a week of discussion, and the three of them went to the UAW headquarters in the Hoffman Building in downtown Detroit. There they met Sam Burlingame, who was in charge of one of the organizing units of the UAW. He signed them up, took their initiation fees, and gave them application cards to take back to the shop. That same week in January Kord, Shannon, and Ptasz recruited Jake Stolz, Joseph Stankosky, and one or two others. It was not easy to convince them, but the unionists were persistent. They hammered away at the numerous grievances—particularly the lack of job security and seniority—and argued that, just as auto workers were doing elsewhere, the workers in the Detroit Parts Company could struggle and win. The Flint sit-down strike was in progress, and it was a good persuader. The whole group, numbering six or seven, went down to headquarters, where Burlingame took their application cards and initiation fees. At this time he told them that there was an organizing office located near the plant on Joseph Campau, the main street of Hamtramck. Morris Field was in charge there, and Burlingame was going to transfer their cards to Field's jurisdiction. Their next contact would be with him.

All of this was done quietly. Cautious and scared, the small group of unionists was aware of its weakness and isolation. These early unionists took some comfort in their lack of notoriety. At most, perhaps one or two of their fellow workers in torch-welding knew what was going on. Yet within a few days of this second contact with Burlingame, J. A. Bergson, the plant manager, came down to torch-welding, went over to the foreman, Bob Toller, and pointed out each member of the union, repeatedly saying, "This S.O.B. is in the union, and this S.O.B. is in the union . . ." He missed no one. Obviously there were spies somewhere in the shop feeding information to the manager. To the early unionists, this seemed the obvious explanation, but it eventually proved to be not the only one.

What was the effect of this act of intimidation? Undoubtedly, it cowed the six or seven nonmembers; if any had been sympathetic before, they would think more than twice now. And the more aggressive workers had already joined. It was unlikely that the union would grow in torch-welding—not at this early stage, at any rate. Yet the effort at intimidation backfired. As the rationale for secrecy and caution had been destroyed by J. A. Bergson, these early unionists became more open and active. It was clear that they could not afford to wait until they mopped up in their own department. Johnny Galinsky, an older first-generation Pole who had been fired by Ford when he passed forty, was terrified of losing his job; Ralph Stubb was the foreman's nephew; Bill Smith, an older northern-born Protestant, was sympathetic, but timid and fearful; Harold Lewis, a migrant of Welsh background from North Dakota, and one of the biggest and most powerful workers in the plant, was unconvinced and insisted that he knew nothing about unions; and Richard Simkins, a young migrant from the hills of North Carolina, was aloof and skeptical. A few others likewise remained distant. "We had to keep up a momentum," Kord recalls. "[We had to] find contacts and possible leaders in nearby departments, convince them, sign them up, and put them to work in their own departments. . . . I believed we could keep moving and hammer while the iron was hot." Thus, cautious efforts were made to contact a few people in the adjacent press departments. Johnny Zyznomyrsky and Frank Jaskiewicz were friendly and sympathetic, but they were isolated among the 115 workers of the press departments.

In the next few weeks the union as far as Kord was aware included this informal group in torch-welding, plus Zyznomyrsky and Jaskiewicz in the press departments. The latter two, however, lacked the determination of Kord and Shannon, and, partly because of their isolation, their activities were minimal. No meetings were held, and decisions were usually made by the three original and most active members—Shannon, Kord, and Leo Ptasz. After the contact with Morris Field they were reporting back to the others, exchanging a few words in the can, at lunch, or in the periods of idleness when there was no work. At this early stage there was little union life. Friendships were not very deep or strong; and it was not along lines of friendship, such as they were, that this early union developed. The decision to become active at this stage was lonely and individualistic. If the militants were persuaded that they would ultimately triumph, their present position was both isolated and perilous. To keep going in the face of this situation a self-interested utilitarianism was hardly sufficient motive. More profound ideals of a broadly democratic nature moved these men. They shared a "resentment of injustice," and if such issues as low pay and insecurity were clearly economic, others, such as forced "loans" to foremen and multiple birthday collections, were humiliations in the deepest sense, striking directly at the integrity of one's personality. This struggle for the Rights of Man and of the Citizen was therefore inseparable from the effort to better wages and working conditions.

The attitudes of J. A. Bergson, Perkins, and Toller, as well as others in the management, were a complex mixture of fear, hostility, confusion, guilt, and sympathy. There was good reason for these feelings. The political order that had seemed so familiar and congenial to entrepreneurs such as Perkins and Bergson seemed to have been shattered by an insurgent mass of workers, immigrants, farmers, liberals, and Reds. Beginning in late 1936 the industrial order—particularly in automobiles—came under siege. And if September 1933 had been bad, that struggle had at least been confined largely to the tool-and-die makers. Now, however, broader masses of workers were on the move, and the first efforts of Kord and Shannon—and of others unknown to them at the other end of the shop—coincided with this second upsurge. The UAW was aggressive and competent; and as the Flint sit-down strike continued, the threat posed by the union seemed ominous. The new labor legislation, the sympathy of Governor Murphy, the activities of Secretary of Labor Frances Perkins, the La Follette committee, and the National Labor Relations Board (NLRB) lent a powerful political and moral support to these early unionists.[15]

Not only was the CIO in close touch with the La Follette committee and the NLRB, but the municipality of Hamtramck itself was strongly pro-union. As early as the spring of 1936 the growing split between conservative anti-union politicians and progressive pro-union forces was resolved in favor of the latter, beginning a process which over the next several years would see the UAW and the political structure of Hamtramck become increasingly intertwined.[16] On March 12, 1936, Rudolph Tenerowicz, candidate for mayor of the progressive forces, sent a letter to Richard Frankensteen (the leader of the union at Dodge) stating his sympathies with the union and affirming that the police would not be used "to drive and escort strike breakers to and from their work."[17] Three of the five council members elected were supporters of Tenerowicz. One of these, Mrs. Mary Zuk, was a member of the liberal labor group called the People's League. In the summer of 1935 Mrs. Zuk had led a successful meat boycott against high prices and thus became the target of an anti-Communist crusade led by a number of parish priests. The churches, which had refused to support the UAW and had even opposed it, now found their political power waning.[18] By the end of the summer of 1936 the mayor and the city council were backing the UAW all the way, calling on Chrysler to recognize the union as the sole bargaining agent for the workers in its plants.[19] Stanley Nowak, special Polish organizer for the UAW, was acquiring the immense popularity that would lead to his election as state senator from the district embracing Hamtramck.[20]

Perkins, the self-made man, was the least ambivalent in this situation. Who the hell did they think they were, telling him how to run his business! But the new legal and political situation limited his freedom of action. He risked a court case, an unfavorable hearing, and direct government intervention if he acted as he had in 1933. And the new political situation in Hamtramck must have been painfully apparent. He would have to find other means of fighting the union. J. A. Bergson, on the other hand, was more complicated. He was a religious man, a leader in his church, and he tried to be a good Christian. Neither harsh nor without his doubts, on a number of occasions he was bewildered; and in the midst of this tense, uncertain situation he felt obliged to do the right thing. Bob Toller, the foreman in torch-welding, was an old Socialist blackballed some years earlier in Reading, Pennsylvania. "He was as good a boss as might be permitted in those days, and he was closer to his men."

The response of the company to the threat of unionism took the form of intimidation and espionage. Bergson's attempt at psychologically terrorizing the group in torch-welding has already been noted. More specific threats were made against Kord. Toller warned him on several occasions that he would be fired if he kept up his activities, finally pointing out that if this happened his family would be deported. This was not Toller's idea: he felt opposed to it but was in effect cowed by Bergson into transmitting these threats. As we have seen before, attempts at intimidation can backfire; and though the threats to Kord scared him, they strengthened his resolve and stimulated him to act more vigorously. In Kord's opinion, these early weeks provided the company with the best opportunity for defeating the union. If Perkins or Bergson had fired a few leaders, they might have eliminated the threat of unionism—at least until the war. "But," says Kord, "the company hesitated and was lost."

The spies—at least those the union suspected—were not necessarily recruited by the company. Certainly some of the setup men in departments 17 and 19 were hostile to the union effort and were reporting back. Predominantly northern-born native Americans, they felt no sympathy toward the Polish workers who operated the presses. Moreover, they were operating a racket in which they would place some of the production earned by the press operators on their own time cards, splitting the take with the foreman. Kord and Shannon had made elimination of this system a major goal of the union and were producing effective propaganda out of it.

Al Schein had already revealed his hostility toward unionism, and his Masonic ties to the foreman were known. Others just wanted to make points with the company, hoping thereby to gain preference and personal advancement. It was easy, after the union had been forced into the open, to feign interest as a means of gathering intelligence.

Field had surprised Kord and Shanon with the information that a group had been organizing in front-welding. He thus proposed that they call a joint meeting of the two groups. Although the unification of these two groups was Field's primary concern, the unionists saw the necessity of gaining a better foothold in the shop. Within prudent limits, therefore, they determined to publicize this meeting. Their position in the plant was precarious, and they felt the pressure. Small and isolated, their group was too easy a target for management reprisals. If they failed quickly to establish a broader base, they would be vulnerable; and failure to grow would only encourage Perkins and Bergson to move against them.

Around the middle of February, Kord, Shannon, and Ptasz began to make more frequent contact with some of the workers in departments 17 and 19. On February 11, the UAW had emerged victorious in its struggle with General Motors. This certainly boosted the morale of the handful of unionists in the Detroit Parts Company and made an impact on the rest of the workers. Yet morale was not easily translated into solid organizational gains. Johnny Zyznomyrsky and Frank Jaskiewicz felt sympathetic and were coming to the meeting, but Kord knew that unless the press departments had a solid nucleus, activity there would be minimal. In building the meeting, therefore, the unionists had to make broader contacts and persuade new people to join. Under these circumstances the set-up men could easily observe what was happening, other unknown self-appointed spies could pick up information, or some of the foremen may have known of the meeting, which was scheduled for an evening in late February or early March. The time and place could hardly be kept secret. That there would be spies at the meeting no one could question; only their numbers remained in doubt.

Thus, when Kord arrived at Joseph Campau he noticed a number of men across the street from the union hall (a room above a bar) closely observing and noting down those entering the building. This was not a large meeting; besides the groups from torch- and front-welding, and Zyznomyrsky and Jaskiewicz[21] from the press departments, there was a scattering of others, including some spies. There were perhaps fifteen or twenty workers present. Kord had known the workers from front-welding only on sight. Now, however, he and his comrades found out who were the unionists among them.

About the same time that Kord and Shannon had begun their activity in torch, John Vasdekis and Leonard Pinkowicz had started organizing in front-welding. Vasdekis, a second-generation Lithuanian, and Pinkowicz, a second-generation Pole, were both welders. While Kord, Shannon, and Ptasz had been contacting the Detroit headquarters of the UAW, Vasdekis and Pinkowicz had gotten in touch directly with Morris Field in the Hamtramck office. In a few weeks they were able to recruit several other workers, among them Ed Ruwalski, known in the plant as "King Kong," a second-generation Polish welder; Bill Lewis. Harold Lewis's brother, a Welsh migrant from North Dakota; William Cooper, originally a migrant from Appalachia, but by now a relatively long-time Northern resident; "Alice the Goon," "Sawdust," and a few others. In all, these early unionists in front-welding numbered about eight or nine. King Kong had earned his nickname not only because of his size, but also because of the thick, black hair that covered his body. Although not as furry, both Bill Lewis and his brother Harold were even bigger. Harold, the smallest of eight children, weighed 240 pounds. This military advantage was important in the struggle to come. On one occasion, for example, Bill Lewis, angered by a procompany stoolie, lifted him off the ground, folded him up like a jackknife, and rammed him into a barrel. It took four men to get him out. Others in the front of the shop—among them Alice the Goon and Sawdust—were nearly as strong.

Prior to the meeting at the hall on Joseph Campau, the group in front-welding had already held a few meetings in Bill Lewis's basement. How much of this the company's men knew about is unclear; that they did know something would be demonstrated in a few weeks, when the deficient state of their intelligence activities would cause their greatest blunder. Although these small groups of unionists had known of each others' existence before the meeting, the event itself inspired a feeling of elation. Nevertheless, they remained suspicious of each other. Field, who acted as chairman, said that there were spies at every meeting of this sort. Either Vasdekis or Shannon announced that he knew who the spies were. "We didn't," Kord recalls, "but two could play this game." Field then explained that he would try to build an organization out of the separate groups and individuals who were already working for unionism.

The workers determined to bring new members to the next meeting, and a number of people agreed to take application cards back to the shop. The question of officers arose, and the decision was made to hold elections at the next meeting, to be held in about two or three weeks. Meanwhile, Kord, who had volunteered to act as secretary on this occasion, had been taking notes. This intensified the suspicions of the front welders. Who was this guy taking notes, this college student who was so different from the other workers? Cautious and wary, they vowed to continue their separate meetings.

The two welding departments were the only centers of union activity, and because of the front welders' distrust of Kord, each group of unionists acted separately and was to some extent unaware of the other's efforts. They were still only a relative handful of perhaps twenty-five out of five hundred workers in the plant. And the front welders were unsure that Kord was not a spy. "We all knew there were spies around," Kord recalls. "Who? Who did you ask to join? Everybody? No. You first ask individuals you are beginning to notice as prospects. But can this guy who starts being friendly possibly want to suck out info or is he trying to tell you he is with you and might sign up if asked? You don't ask everybody; [and] there starts to be some prestige in being asked. You may be asked not only to join but to lead in your department."

Nevertheless, the joint meeting was "a shot in the arm." The union had not only grown larger but was functioning more effectively. There was "more excitement, satisfaction, and hope." "More people" were contacted "more often and more openly." A primitive network of communication emerged. Vasdekis, King Kong, and Cooper began to visit the contiguous departments, sometimes getting as far as department 19, while Kord and Shannon were in touch with the middle of the shop. These visits lasted for less than five minutes and occurred about once a day. Shannon, though, ranged further more frequently and stayed longer on his propaganda excursions. The emissaries from the front-welding department sometimes met Kord or Shannon in department 19. Such contacts had their effect, and other workers were encouraged to join. In the future these early joiners would become secondary leaders of the union.

In the few weeks following the first joint meeting the isolation and loneliness among the unionists began to break down. People spoke to each other more frequently, particularly in the neighborhood bars that were across the street from the plant. Members and nonmembers mingled and discussed the events of the day, and it was in the bars that some of the new members were recruited. In addition to having recruited Zyznomyrsky and Jaskiewicz in the press departments, the union gained a foothold in the toolroom with the adherence of Fred Luebke and Bert Robertson to the organization.

At this stage both the hopes of the union and the fears of the company began to center on the press departments. It was becoming obvious to Kord and the others that with Schein holding back the inspection department, with the toolroom either hostile or indifferent, and with shipping separated from the pro-union part of the shop by the inspection department, their strategy had to aim toward a buildup of strength in the center of the shop. Not only were the press departments contiguous to torch-welding, but a large portion of the press operators were young second-generation Poles. If there was any hope of expansion it rested with them. The first-generation immigrants, even those few who had been Socialists, were, if sympathetic, deeply fearful.

Among the northern-born native Americans only one or two were active, and while a few more were friendly but afraid, the rest remained either aloof or hostile.

The company feared the ability of the unionists to talk to the press operators, who according to Kord were the most easily accessible and who "had the right psychology." What the union saw as a weak nucleus in these departments the company viewed with alarm. Both Zyzno-myrsky and Jaskiewicz were good secondary leaders. They had courage, initiative, and determination. To Perkins and Bergson, the success of the UAW in Flint had inspired morbid fears. Yet Flint was sixty miles northwest of Hamtramck. By March, however, the sit-down wave not only had engulfed Detroit, but in many ways seemed to be a more serious and threatening upheaval than the recently concluded Flint strike.[22] And on March 8, the whole Chrysler Corporation was hit by a massive sit-down. "With several thousand workers inside the plants and over 100,000 idled by the automobile stoppage; with 30 other sitdowns taking place in the city and the Teamsters ready to quit in sympathy, Detroit felt imperilled by a general strike."[23] On March 23, the UAW called a mammoth rally in Cadillac Square. The Dodge local was influential in the selection of such Hamtramck officials as the chief of police, and the police department itself was sympathetic to the workers. Trapped in the middle of the staunchly pro-union municipality, the management of Detroit Parts Company must have felt helpless.[24]

To head off the possibility that Zyznomrysky and Jaskiewicz would gain a following in the press departments, the management, fearful of any direct confrontation, hit upon a sociological stratagem. Soon after the joint meeting they began to hire young second-generation Poles just out of high school. Although the second-generation workers already employed in the press departments were young, these new workers were a few years younger. The differences between them in outlook and experience were great, and the company hoped that the youth and inexperience of these new workers as well as their desire to hold a job, would thwart the organizational work of the union.

By the time of the second meeting, the union had augmented its ranks by about 50 percent, but its overall situation had changed relatively little. Most of its growth was confined to the front-welding department, while a few people joined in the press departments, and perhaps Zero in cutoff and Wilson in transportation joined (although Kord is not sure; they may have joined a few weeks later).

The meeting, held in March, was concerned chiefly with the election of officers. Bert Robertson, a loud and aggressive machine repairman, had made a good reputation for himself. He had come into the shop in January. No one knew much about him, but he appeared to know about unions, and seemed to be fearless. Whereas others were still relatively cautious, he would travel around the shop—his work required plant-wide mobility—noisily talking about the union and handing out cigars, which he always carried with him. Although he did not join until after the first meeting, he quickly became known as a bold union spokesman. Moreover, he was the only unionist able to move about freely, and the others got to know him better than anyone else from outside their own departments. In spite of Robertson's verbal militancy, though, he was doing little organizing. Given the naïveté of these early unionists and the lack of significant criteria at this time, the choice for president seemed obvious. Robertson was nominated and elected unopposed. Shannon was elected vice-president, Vasdekis financial secretary, and Pinkowicz secretary. Bill Lewis, the strongest man in the shop, was chosen for sergeant at arms.

# CHAPTER TWO

# Early Confrontations

## Breakthrough: The Second-Generation Poles

ON A DAY late in April 1937 the situation in torch-welding was as follows: the union was at an impasse, although there was no hostility or tension between union members and the others in the department. Kord, Shannon, and Ptasz had continued their efforts to persuade the others (except, for obvious reasons, the foreman's nephew). They had hammered away at all that was wrong in the shop—the lack of seniority, the uncertainty of being called back after layoffs, the absence of grievance procedures, and the inadequate wage rates. Repeatedly, they had pointed to the sit-downs sweeping the automobile industry as examples of what determined workers could accomplish. All of the non-union workers in the department had agreed with this general bill of grievances, but Simpkins, known as Hillbilly, thought that unions went too far and might be short-lived; Lewis knew nothing about unions; Galinsky was afraid he would be unable to get another job if he was fired from this one; and Smith was fearful. Others also responded with a mixture of fear and doubt; they would wait and see.

It was perhaps two in the afternoon. Through his informants, J. A. Bergson had discovered that secret meetings were being held in Lewis's basement. From what followed, it was apparent that either he was misinformed or he simply did not know which Lewis brother was the culprit. At any rate, Bergson had decided to make his move, and Harold Lewis, in torch-welding, was the target.

[As Kord relates, Bergson] first went to Toller and talked to him for a few minutes. Then he went over to where Harold was sitting. Lewis was just learning welding at the time—he was also the saw man. Bergson stood for a while observing. He wasn't much taller standing than Lewis

22

was sitting. Then he made some critical remark and got no response. Quiet for a while—another remark. By then Shannon and I felt [that] something was up. This continued for a while—no response. The department became aware. Some of the work noises stopped, some people—all the grinders—stopped work and witnessed. Now you could get the drift much better. Galinsky and Toller's nephew worked but observed over glasses—wary expressions. Hillbilly stopped—smiling—what's going on happen now—who'll win this one? Leo Ptasz stopped—his usual enigmatic half smile. J. A. said that if Lewis were concerned with his work instead of organizing a union and holding meetings in his basement he would do a much better job. The gist of this was heard by everyone. All this time, and now too, Lewis didn't even look at him. He stopped work, put out his torch, hung it up, then took off his goggles, [and] stood up, up, up! Involuntarily J. A. moved. Lewis took a couple of steps up to me and said, "Hey Professor! Give me one of those goddamn applications!"

Joe [Stankosky] laughed, Shannon had a mischievous, amused smile. I didn't crack a smile, gave him the application and he started filling it out. Bill had to sit there—sheepish. The rest observed with no change [of] expression, but all [work] had stopped. People in [department] 19 nearby had noticed something afoot and they had stopped, looked, not knowing exactly what [had] happened. J. A. walked away without another word, [while] Lewis [was] signing his application. Buzzing and movement started first in 19. Word spread like wildfire—some came to us for details, others moved to other parts of 19 and into 17.

This was as much as I caught—it was pure drama. Afterward there was a lot of movement, short excited exchanges. I got none of the conversation. I was signing up Lewis. I didn't say much or do much of anything. This was being done by others. I played it cool; it was much more effective to let the floodwaters roll for a while.

It couldn't have happened any better. [Bergson] had to quietly walk through 19. Think how he felt—guys standing there watching—not working; laughing—not scared.

We knew we could gain important new ground but we also had to brace ourselves for a possible company response—this never came in any dangerous form. All of a sudden we won some kind of a showdown. The company backed off, others were spreading the good tidings—all we had to do was gather in another layer of members in the next few days. Later in the day we were visited by some of the leaders in the front-welding department—word reached them fast.

"Harold Lewis's dramatic entry into the union . . . electrified the other sections of the shop." News of the incident spread rapidly, and, although the union did not expand into inspection, maintenance, the toolroom, or swaging, there was a substantial increase in membership in the departments where organization had already existed. The activists still had to take the initiative and approach prospective members—few workers ever spontaneously joined—but recruitment was easier. In the next few weeks activity increased, the members became more open and optimistic, and there was greater cohesion. Moreover, new leadership was emerging, seeking advice from Kord and Shannon.

For the first time the unionists were interacting more directly in a broader and more complex social milieu. With a substantial nucleus among the press operators and with a foothold in department 18, different cultural and psychological currents appeared which had hitherto been veiled by their inactivity. Whether or not people were union members, they began to appear as individuals acting in a some-times tense, sometimes dramatic situation.

Among the unionists in torch-welding "feelings of strength and confi-dence shot up." Yet in this department only one or two workers joined the union. The others, including Hillbilly, Bill Smith, Johnny Galinsky, and the foreman's nephew, Ralph Stubb, held back, still fearful and unconvinced. The union would have to show greater strength, and the company greater weakness, before they would commit themselves. Thus, in the department where the dramatic action had just taken place and where the company had been dealt its most serious defeat so far, the immediate palpable impact was slight.

In departments 16 (swaging) and 18 (cutoff) organization consis-tently lagged behind that of the press departments. Cutoff was larger than swaging, and slightly less than half of the workers were second-generation Poles. In the cutoff department Zero, a second-generation Pole, and a few others of similar background supplied the union with its foothold. At this time Zero was about twenty-five years old, was married, and sometimes hung out in bars. He had impressed Kord as "more rational" than most of the other workers; "he was not one of the volatile ones." Zero, a serious Catholic, looked to Pinkowicz for leadership, and from the start the cutoff department came under the direct influence of the two major leaders in front-welding.

By now the union had gained a toehold in the transportation department. The workers in this department were responsible for moving stock around inside the plant. Both hand trucks and power-driven forklifts were used. The power-truck drivers were mostly second generation, although there were a few Appalachians. These drivers were more skilled than the others in their department and traveled more extensively in the plant. The hand truck operators were largely older, first-generation Poles. The department consisted of twenty or twenty-five workers who were attached to specific departments and who generally traveled in regular circuits in the plant. The transportation department was thus somewhat fictitious, carrying a name mainly for bookkeeping purposes. The most active unionist in transportation was Elmer Wilson. Married, about twenty-five, a committed Catholic of native American background, Wilson would quickly become one of the major secondary leaders in the local.

Most of the workers in the shipping department were first generation who were engaged in heavy labor, loading and unloading trucks. Early support for the union in this department came from Lew Thompson, a northern-born black, and Frenchy LeSante, a French Canadian. It is not clear whether they were union members at this time. Two other blacks in the department made up the rest of the precontract union supporters (although even here it is not absolutely certain that they joined before the contract). In addition, it is possible that there were one or two second-generation Poles in the department, and they may have been early supporters. Both Frenchy, who drove a truck, and Thompson, who used mechanical packing devices, were paid slightly more than the loaders. Because of the social composition of shipping and its location between two large blocs of anti-union workers, the union remained small and relatively stagnant in this department.

That shipping was cracked at all at this time reflected the union's growing mobility and the expansion of its network of communications. The six unionists that regularly traveled around the shop increased to twelve, with Jaskiewicz, Wilson, Zyznomyrsky and three others joining Kord, Shannon, Vasdekis, King Kong, Cooper, and others. The visits themselves became somewhat lengthened and may have increased in frequency. The adherence of Wilson to the union had important strategic implications. As he drove his power truck around the plant, Wilson's orbit included shipping, department 19, and torch-welding. This route provided an important means of communication in the early days and may have been the only contact the union regularly had with the shipping department (although Shannon might have gotten that far).

Young second-generation workers predominated in the front-welding department and the press departments. It was among them that the union had its roots and upon them that its hopes for success depended. Yet at the outset it was primarily the welders among them who provided initiative and support. They were, among the generally young second generation, the oldest group. They were all married and of the production workers had the longest seniority. Their ties to the neighborhood gangs had dissolved—marriage usually marked the disintegration of gang life, the dissolution of neighborhood communal solidarity, and the emergence of a more individuated existence. The extended family was weakened and tradition gave way to rationalism and self-improvement. In a milieu where drinking was not only heavy and extensive, but also a measure of one's manhood, these workers, with the exception of the group around Vasdekis, drank relatively little. They were the most highly skilled production workers (they did their own setup work), and if considerably below the skill level of the men in the toolroom, their work required training, discipline, and responsibility.

Among the helpers in front-welding somewhat under 50 percent were second generation. Although the position of helper was unskilled, the second generation among the helpers had expectations of improvement. "To stay a helper anybody would do. But new welders would also have to be found among helpers, so you needed more than first generation," Kord notes. Such a striving for advancement implied more than a desire for higher pay. Many of the qualities of discipline and responsibility mentioned in regard to welders were also present in these helpers. They had relatively greater stability on the job, most of them were married, and they were a couple of years older than the press operators. In the aftermath of the Lewis incident the strength of the union among these second-generation helpers was significantly greater than that among the second-generation press operators. With few exceptions the first generation among the helpers remained fearful and inactive. However much their sympathy may have been with the second-generation unionists, they gave no support until after the contract.

In the two press departments, the social composition of the workers was about as follows:

|  | Department | |
| --- | --- | --- |
|  | 19 | 17 |
| Second generation | | |
| New hires | 25% | 20% |
| Earlier hires | 50% | 60% |
| First generation | | |
| Poles | 10% | 10% |
| Ukrainians | A few | A few |
| Russians and Lithuanians | 2 | None that Kord remembers |

The first-generation immigrants among these workers in the two press departments were in most respects similar to the other first-generation workers in the plant. On the other hand, in spite of the similarity of background and a difference of only a few years of age, the two groups of second-generation workers in the press departments—the new hires and the earlier hires—possessed dissimilar expectations of their situation, related differently to the foremen, and responded variously to the appeals of the union.

For the new hires working here was their first job. They were unmarried, lived at home, and did not have to support a household (although they contributed to the family income). In relation either to their needs or to their past experience they thought their wages high. Working in the plant was itself an adventure. Moreover, throughout Hamtramck loose territorial gangs formed a fairly ubiquitous matrix of youthful fraternity. These gangs were basically benevolent in nature: their activities were mainly recreational, although there occurred some minor disturbances, fights over leadership, and infrequent petty crime. When the company had begun the policy of hiring teenage workers, intelligence to this effect had spread along the lines of gang associations in the neighborhood of the plant. One gang member would get a job in the Detroit Parts Company and pass the word along, and others would follow. They lived in the neighborhood, within walking distance of the plant. Consequently this wave of new workers was to a great extent composed of a number of subgroups drawn from the several neighborhood gangs. Whether the company was aware of this is not clear, but in a plant where the workers were mostly strangers to each other, these people had had many contacts among themselves before they started to work. These young Poles thus brought into the press departments a ready-made social infrastructure whose basic attributes included loyalty and solidarity.

The slightly older second-generation workers in the press departments (the earlier hires) were likewise members of gangs; in this case, however, the gangs were slowly breaking up. These workers had had a longer experience with the company and with working conditions. They had girls and were planning to get married, or they were already married. They were on their own, and yet they knew that for press operators the chances of being rehired after a layoff were no better than fifty-fifty. They were far more hostile toward the company, yet their behavior in relation to the foremen was more circumspect, less brazen than that of the new hires.

Before the Lewis incident the union nucleus in the press departments was composed entirely of the earlier hires, and although Kord and Shannon "were glad to see in the new hires a don't-give-a-damn attitude," they "looked for leadership" in the earlier hires. In the immediate aftermath of the Lewis incident Jaskiewicz and Zyznomrysky were activated. "We gained ground [in the press departments, 17 and 19] fast, more people were a lot more openly friendly. People we didn't know knew us and showed it. Seventeen and 19 acquired a substantial new membership—young still—there was a kind of elation among them."

The influx of press operators which followed the Lewis incident was still relatively small; in these departments the union had signed up only 15 to 20 percent of the workers. Moreover, this first breakthrough in the middle of the shop involved mainly the slightly older earlier hires—people in their early twenties. The new hires at first did not take the union's organizing effort seriously, and their understanding of it was relatively superficial. "The new hires understood the idea of union but it was less real and they had less conviction." They were, however, less cowed by the company, though their brazenness had something of an individualistic, even nihilistic, character. They were rebellious, resentful of discipline—even mischievous. When one of them was making his required production report at the end of his shift, "he reported 'two barrels and a box.' This was funny; he obviously wasn't impressed by the company. We all got the humor and enjoyed the frustration of the foreman: he sputtered, that's all."

Those workers who were active in the union during the month of March, immediately following the second joint meeting, possessed a number of social characteristics which distinguished them not only from the broader numbers of inactive workers, but also from the militants who would enter the union in the next eight weeks (April and May). Most striking at the outset is the diversity of their backgrounds. Kord (the "professor"), an intellectual from an urban, anticlerical, Socialist family, immediately stands out among his fellow Poles, who were uneducated and were either peasants (as were the immigrants) or the sons of peasants. Shannon, described earlier, was the only man in the shop with any trade-union background and may well have been the only worker of Irish extraction. Vasdekis, a Lithuanian whom Kord described as more intelligent and more self-educated than the other workers, possessed considerable ability and was both aggressive and decisive. He had moved from Buffalo, and as far as Kord remembers he had little family in Detroit: he himself lived not in Hamtramck but in Ferndale, a less ethnic, more mixed community. At one time, Kord believes, Vasdekis had been involved on the fringes of radical activity—perhaps in the Communist-led unemployed movement. He was married and drank in moderation. Pinkowicz, although Polish, exhibited a striking peculiarity which set him apart from the other second-generation Poles: whereas in relation to the church the latter were either apathetic or merely nominal church members, Pinkowicz was both a devout believer and an active participant in church affairs. (Immediately after the war he organized a chapter of the Association of Catholic Trade Unionists and launched an unsuccessful struggle against the Socialist leadership of Kord, Shannon, and others, although this never developed into a permanent division or split.) Pinkowicz, a "deliberate thinker," was "slow to excite." "Deeply moral" and possessed of "great integrity," he was looked to for leadership by virtue of the respect he commanded. In spite of his deep sense of religious morality he "mostly accepted others despite their failings." His morality was personal, although he did show silent disapproval of Shannon's "lapses from grace."

Within the front-welding group, Vasdekis was the principal personality. King Kong, William Cooper, Bill Lewis, Alice the Goon, and Sawdust clustered around him, accepting his leadership without question. In some ways Vasdekis shared their fierceness, their militancy, and their tendency to use violence as a solution to every problem. Yet if this made Vasdekis congenial to them, it was his discipline, his ability to think things out better than they, and his broader view of things that won their respect and even subservience. Pinkowicz, on the other hand, had no such rapport with them and in the absence of Vasdekis would never have been able to take his place and become the center of the group. In this respect he was an outsider. Yet he had great influence on Vasdekis himself. Vasdekis was aware, Kord thinks, of his tendency to respond intemperately and violently to problems, and he accepted Pinkowicz's moderating influence as a valuable counterbalance to his own impulses. Thus, Pinkowicz had a strong but indirect influence on the whole group. In addition, he became an informal representative of a certain Catholic element in the plant.

Kord was the key personality in the Shannon, Jaskiewicz, Zyznomyrsky, Ptasz, and Wilson group. A number of characteristics distinguished this body of men from the Vasdekis group. Although Shannon had greater popularity in the shop and was more prominent than Kord, the latter played the unifying role within the torch, press, transportation group. The group itself was much less closely knit than the Vasdekis group. In the latter, the ties were fraternal, extending outside the shop into the bars and in fact into a whole mode of existence which encompassed a lot of street activity, including barroom brawling. The Kord group, however, was not only much more temperate, but more ideological and more individualistic as well.

It is important to note the distinctions between the secondary leaders in the Vasdekis group and those in the Kord group. In terms of the degree of involvement and capability, in terms of the range of their activities and the greater breadth of their understanding, the Kord group of secondary leaders occupied a significantly more advanced position. To understand this difference it is necessary to anticipate the events of the next two years. In that time the Kord group developed rapidly. It expanded in numbers and influence, establishing itself not only in the three original departments where it began—torch and the two press departments—but also in swaging, inspection, and especially the toolroom. Over a few years the entire group was recruited by Kord into the Socialist party. New leadership was attracted to Kord. Among them were Walter Adams, a Polish inspector who would later become president of the local; Elmer Wilson, the power-truck driver who in 1938 went into the toolroom; and a number of workers who would become stewards and committeemen, including Harry Kozik, George Kiertanis, and Frenchy LeSante.

On the other hand, the Vasdekis group remained unchanged, never extending its influence beyond front-welding. King Kong, Bill Lewis, and William Cooper became stewards in their own department. Yet their leadership possessed a different character from that of Jaskiewicz, Zyznomyrsky, Wilson, and the others in the Kord group. Johnny Zyznomyrsky, for example, one of the lesser secondary leaders in the Kord group (in contrast to both Wilson and Jaskiewicz who were more active on a plant-wide basis and were more involved with problems of local leadership), "was a much more capable steward and union man" than King Kong. "We depended on these guys for muscle." "With the front guys mere size had something to do with" their role and prominence in the union. They liked to brawl, drank heavily, and in their group loyalty, lack of political consciousness, and readiness to go into battle, they seemed to be a more disciplined version of the wildcat type that we will see later. To a great extent it was Vasdekis who provided the discipline and the perspective that enabled them to play an important role early in the union struggle. From the outset it was apparent that the Vasdekis group was "not going to go that far in shouldering responsibility for the union" and were destined to play a diminishing role in the local.

Both as an organization and as a way of life the union began to

unfold its human potential. The Lewis incident had irretrievably dam-
aged the relationships of authority and the mood of fear in the plant.
Sullen isolation was giving way to more open and comradely relationships. Friendships sprang up; workers gathered after work or after
union meetings at the local bars—although the unionists from torch-
welding "never became very bar-minded." The back room of Sharkey's
Bar and Grill was thrown open to the union for special meetings at any
time, whether of small groups or leaders. Unionists visited each other at
home. After the Lewis incident the atmosphere among the unionists
was transformed. Formerly, they had dared to hope; now they could
see ultimate victory within their grasp.

With the dramatic confrontation of the Lewis incident

things started tilting our way. The company was making mistakes; we
never did, but we took advantage of theirs. . . . We—the leadership—
deliberately tried to create the image of strength, success, and confidence, and no doubt this helped some people to join. . . . We were
discussing ways of cracking the holdout departments in general terms in
April; and in May we were talking contract, recognition, seniority,
grievance procedure, representation, and money. Money was the least
important at this time to the leaders, but we knew we had to get some.
Actually, the other things are the guts that make it possible to talk
economics effectively.

Toward this end a bargaining committee was set up in April or May.
Included on it were Robertson, Shannon, Vasdekis, Pinkowicz, Luebke,
and perhaps one more. Luebke's inclusion was a political maneuver: the
leadership hoped through this representation of the few toolroom unionists on the leading committees to break down the resistance in that
department. On the other hand, although Kord had become advisor,
strategist, and planner to the others in the shop, he had no desire to
take on added duties. His responsibilities toward his family and the
desire to finish college led him to think of himself more as a persuader
than as a leader.

The growth of the union after the Lewis incident had taken the form
of an influx of new members in the first week. In the next two or three
weeks, however, this growth tapered off sharply, and a period of

relative stagnation set in. To the leadership it became clear that unless this early organizing momentum was maintained, a decline would set in. The union had a bare majority in torch-welding; less than a majority in front-welding; 15 to 20 percent in the press departments; perhaps 15 percent in the cutoff department; two workers in the toolroom; one or two workers in transportation; one or two workers in shipping; and nothing in inspection.

The company, however, took a different view of the situation. By the late spring of 1937, the strike-wave had already inundated the industrial landscape. Following the Flint victory and the Chrysler sit-down the organization drive seemed like an irresistible tide. Membership growth was spectacular: 88,000 in February 1937, 166,000 in March, and 254,000 in April. By October it would reach 400,000. In the weeks following the April 6 settlement with Chrysler the UAW secured agreements from Hudson, Reo, Packard, Studebaker, and numerous parts producers.[1] Richard Frankensteen has noted "how fast [the oranizational drive] was moving and how much fear the companies had of the flying squadrons. They were all scared stiff that they were going to be chosen the next day as the one that would be closed."[2] Inspired by such fears and unable to fathom the Slavic mind of the mass of workers, the Detroit Parts Company sought to steal the union's thunder. Where the fear of the stick had failed, perhaps the lure of the dangling carrot might succeed.

## The Breakdown of Authority

On a day in May some three or four weeks after the Lewis incident, the company determined on a new tactic. The foremen, under instructions from the management, called the workers into their offices one at a time and confidentially told each one that he was getting a five-cent raise for his loyalty to the company. An effort was made to create the impression that only he or a few like him were so favored.

Perhaps if there had been some measure of cultural homogeneity and solidarity, some similarity in religious and ethnic background, or if both entrepreneurs and workers had coexisted for generations in a stable community, this effort to bolster loyalty might have succeeded. As it happened, there was no loyalty to bolster, no communal solidarity to reinforce. The company had again failed to estimate correctly the temper of the sons of Hamtramck's Polish immigrants. On this day the effort to create a sense of confidentiality and grateful submissiveness backfired. Word spread through the shop, scathing remarks were exchanged, and the company was ridiculed. "There was immediate recognition of the fact that this was a sign of indecision, confusion, and weakness. Somehow we [the leadership] didn't have to work to bring this out. One of the new hires asked out loud, 'If I get my buddy to join do I get another raise?' "

The unionists were jubilant. They had correctly taken the psychological measure of the company, preying on its fears and successfully leading the whole plant to accept an exaggerated—but never specific—estimate of the union's strength. Vasdekis held the membership cards and he alone knew the real strength of the union, although Kord, Shannon, and Pinkowicz probably had a good idea of the truth. The rest of the workers, however, both union and non-union, believed the organization to be stronger than it was. "If the company had known how weak we were . . . they might [have tried] something other than a five-cent raise." Everyone else in the plant was jolted; the odds began to shift. The older second-generation press operators now figured that the union might well succeed; the new hires were betting on a winner; the first generation was emerging from its shell of fear and realizing that the union had strength after all; and the remaining non-unionists in torch-welding saw that at least it was an even match.

The excitement that followed was rooted in something more profound: as the company began to exhibit fear and indecisiveness and as the union began to act with greater confidence, the prevailing structures of authority began to crumble. As a result of the company's display of weakness, the unionists now scored major gains in the press departments among both the new hires and the older second-generation workers. Yet even here the strength of the union rose only to 25 to 30 percent. The new hires listened and were friendly; some joined and some said they would join later "when my buddy does." There were no discussions about the union, but the activists did not see them as a major obstacle. The slightly older second-generation workers continued to be organizationally more responsive.

Among the new hires who now joined the union, a curious phenomenon was observed by Kord. Some of them who worked close together and were probably gang members appeared to join the union in groups. Especially in department 19, there appeared to be small closely knit groups of workers. "They would have lunch together, would leave the shop together. There seemed to be a correlation—today none in the union, tomorrow four or five join. Things were done to some extent in such groups. And department 19 seemed more volatile than 17; it seemed to have more of this gang spirit. More workers in this department seemed to belong to gangs . . . and it seemed also that the union enjoyed somewhat greater support in this department than in 17." Yet following this rapid surge, which occurred over a matter of days, "there were no more group joinings after a while. We had to convince them and sign them up one at a time. Sometimes they asked who is already in, is so-and-so in." "Groups," notes Kord, "were very important in getting things moving." Such groups existed as well among the slightly older second-generation press operators, and there too the group phenomenon was to some extent operative, although the groups themselves were further along on the path to ultimate extinction. Most of these group joinings were based on gang ties, but others may have been rooted in the work situation. Kord notes that a crew working together might have joined as a body.

The union now gained a foothold in department 16. Here the workers were mostly immigrants, almost half of them Ukrainian. Kord notes that among these older Ukrainians and Poles traces of the old national antagonisms may have persisted, although given the inactivity of the first generation of both nationalities, this had little impact on the organizing effort. Here only Nick Buglaj, a first-generation Ukrainian, and perhaps one or two second-generation Poles were involved. Although this department was closer to front-welding, Buglaj immediately became close friends with Kord. Through Buglaj the unionists in department 16 were influenced by the strong leadership of Kord and Shannon in torch-welding. Buglaj, "probably of peasant stock," had "little formal education and was a bit stubborn." He was considerably less active than Zero in the cutoff department, whose involvement Kord described as "a quiet pulling together of those around him." In turn, Zero was considerably less active than Zyznomyrsky and Jaskiewicz in the press departments. The swaging department may have been the worst place to work: the intense noise had partially deafened most of the workers.

The ranks of the union in front-welding still did not include all of the second generation, although there was a strong probability that a majority would join. Growth elsewhere was scattered; one or two workers joined in department 18, as did John Novak, a Slovak Communist in the toolroom. Novak's work as a die setter brought him in close contact with department 17 and the swagers, where he was "apparently able to get along pretty good with the old Poles and Ukrainians," and "had some effect on the first generation."

The aftermath of the five-cent raise, so obviously a result of the company's ill-conceived tactic, further unsettled Patterson and Bergson. "The foremen thought the five-cent raise would cut the union drive. Since Bergson held foremen's meetings from time to time where these things were cooked up, I assume management was of that opinion. They were all surprised that the raise had the opposite effect. Each incident demoralized them further." They were already allowing their fears and imagination to magnify the size and strength of the union; such was the union leadership's strategy, and so far their success in this regard was remarkable. The company now exhibited signs of a genuine loss of mastery and a paralysis of will. "Confused and uncertain," the company "didn't seem to know how to respond." The union leaders "came on strong, daring to face the company." "Some of the secondary leadership and activists were defiant, and in the departments where the union was strong the foremen were backing off and being less aggressive. . . . I imagine the foremen were getting chewed out for not preventing and counteracting the union," Kord suggests. The balance of power was shifting fast; there was something loose and potentially explosive in the situation. A tumult was building that threatened to shatter what was left of the old relationship of authority. Since the Lewis incident, J. A. Bergson, as plant manager the primary representative and embodiment of managerial authority, had not been much in evidence.

Yet the union was not as strong as the company believed, and the leaders knew something that the company did not: the first generation, sympathetic as they were, were not moving; the workers in the tool-room remained hostile or aloof, even though in this department the union had an outpost of three members; and Al Schein was holding back the workers in inspection. It was becoming clear that these were major problem areas. Although the leadership hoped to gain a majority as a means of getting a contract, organization had naturally slowed down after the initial influx following the five-cent raise. Paradoxically, with each burst of activity and broadening of organization the limits of this expansion were becoming all too clear—with some exceptions, only the second-generation workers were joining. The leadership realized the necessity of aggressive psychological warfare and the need for secrecy: no one must know the real strength of the union. Under these circumstances the role of leadership was crucial. "Until a decisive battle is won, fear and uncertainty [remain], and the leaders have to *plan* to maintain some momentum. [They] have to constantly get new ideas for minor gains here and there, [they] have to *plan* to keep the company in a state of imbalance and uncertainty and build strength and confidence in members."

In the few weeks following the five-cent raise the unionists realized that they were approaching some sort of showdown. Union activity intensified. The back room of the bar was much in use and people were "pepping themselves up in the front." Fraternization in the bars was growing. At meetings the workers gave vent to their hostility and built up their courage, "blasting the company and dragging down its stature." Under these circumstances, getting a contract became important in itself, apart from the specific concessions that might be contained in it. "And we had to lie a bit about our numerical strength—[and] even a bit more than that. How can you get people into a fighting mood if you admit weakness?" There was no question anymore: the leadership knew that "a breakthrough was needed or we might not make it in the end." In the next few weeks they had to make a drive for a contract.

# CHAPTER THREE

# Offensive

## The Battle of the Buttons

IN THE AFTERMATH of the five-cent raise, torch-welding had become the only completely organized department. As early as April Kord, Shannon, and Ptasz realized that if they could get their department solidly in the union they would be in a position to carry through a qualitatively more effective struggle. Up until the five-cent raise Galinsky, Bill Smith, and Toller's nephew, Ralph Stubb, had remained fearful and had not joined; and Hillbilly was aloof, argumentative, and unconvinced. After the five-cent raise the situation loosened up. By depicting the strength of the union as greater than it really was, by concentrating on Bill Smith and Ralph Stubb (both of whom were more likely to join), and by applying peer-group pressure, the activists in the department convinced Smith and Stubb to sign up. Stubb was not overly difficult, and Smith joined, fear and all, but it was with reluctance and out of deference to the others that they did so. Circumstances had forced them into a role they had not sought. Elsewhere in the shop people such as they would be among the last to join the union. With Stubb and Smith in, Kord and Shannon turned to Galinsky and Hillbilly. The latter saw the wave of the future and joined. Galinsky was sympathetic but paralyzed by fear. "We were using our numbers as persuasion," remembers Kord. "We told [Galinsky] most everyone was in, [that] there was no longer need of fear. Several people talked to him, but there was no intimidation." And Galinsky joined.

Kord and Shannon realized that they had to utilize this opportunity. During a strategy discussion between them, therefore, the idea came up of a demonstration of power. If all the workers in their department came marching into the plant wearing union buttons, they reasoned, they would create a shock wave like that which had followed the Lewis incident. It would depend on planning and timing, but the intention was clear: to inspire an escalation of activity and militancy in the broader mass of union members by creating an impression of discipline, militancy, and numerical strength. They could then enter into negotiations on a contract and have a reasonable chance of bluffing their way through, for although they still hoped to gain a majority, the chances of doing so appeared increasingly remote. Their attention turned toward their own department.

As far back as March Kord, Vasdekis, Pinkowicz, and a few others had been wearing UAW buttons. The foremen were against this practice, and Kord himself was "talked to" several times. Most of the workers stayed away from the button wearers; it was too dangerous to be seen talking to them. After the Lewis incident a few more militants were wearing buttons, mostly in the welding departments: in torch-welding Kord, Shannon, Leo Ptasz, Stolz, and Harold Lewis; in front-welding Vasdekis, Pinkowicz, Bill Lewis, King Kong, Cooper, Alice the Goon, Sawdust, and perhaps one or two others. But up to this time only those workers who had stuck their necks out as unionists early in the game were sticking their necks out as button wearers, and these were men mostly of leadership and cadre caliber. No rank-and-file union members would have dared to wear buttons at this time. After the five-cent raise, however, button-wearing had become more widespread. Those who did so were still mostly the leadership, some activists, and those who were just "defiant." And some of the new hires— who had not even joined the union—were wearing buttons. It was adventurous, daring, and fun. "We encouraged that," recalls Kord. Wearing buttons in the shop had an important effect on the other union members, helping to wear down their fears. When Kord and Shannon were discussing the prospects for a major demonstration, a few more buttons had begun to appear in department 19; again, among the wearers were a few new hires who were not members of the union. In torch-welding the others were joined by Joseph Stankosky; Shannon's half brother; and, a couple of times in fun, Hillbilly.

There was no general discussion of Kord and Shannon's proposal. There was no consultation.

We talked the idea over first with the more active and militant [unionists in torch-welding], and kept getting a greater degree of agreement; then there just seemed to be a majority decision to sell to the rest. Lewis was enthusiastic and was a good convincer. The last four joiners, however, were reluctant. Galinsky didn't know if it was a good idea or not, but he went along with the idea. Bill Smith and Ralph Stubb would go along if we thought that was the thing to do, and Hillbilly supposed it was OK.

The decision was thus arrived at in an informal way. "We got a majority accord with no trouble and then just took them in order of feasibility down to the weakest link. There was no direct intimidation, but we used Lewis's size effectively. . . . The minority probably felt under group pressure. . . . There was a good degree of solidarity and cohesion. This was very important; they all wanted acceptance." Kord and Shannon also pointed out that "the die was cast," that they "had already stuck their necks out. . . . We tried to impress them with the importance of this act. So far, the company [had not] countered any of our acts effectively. . . . We lied a bit, saying that nothing could possibly happen, that we had the company on the run."

The roots of the solidarity and discipline that would make a demonstration feasible went deeper; such a vanguard action as was now planned would have to depend to some extent on a combination of commitment, loyalty, and peer pressure. And to the last minute, Kord was not sure whether Galinsky would go through with it. But there was a deeper process unfolding, none the less real for its apparent lack of manifest signs. To these few holdouts, incomprehensible changes had taken place in the last several weeks. A handful of workers who in January had seemed doomed to early retirement had mounted an offensive against the company the success of which was all the more mysterious for its dependence not on obvious strength, but on an impalpable and effective form of psychological terror. Kord and Shannon had tempted fate, yet they always came out on top. After each confrontation groups of workers had increasingly shown contempt for the company, had ridiculed the plant manager, and had laughed in his presence. They had joined the union in larger numbers and nothing had happened! There was something almost miraculous in these developments. "Everything we touched showed some degree of success," Kord notes. "We knew when and where to touch."

The personalities of Kord, Shannon, and Lewis seemed endowed with great power. The Lewis incident—the most dramatic reversal the company had suffered—had been elaborated into a local folktale. In the torch-welding department itself there emerged a powerful trio that was now asking for their support and promising protection ("we lied a bit, saying nothing could possibly happen, we had the company on the run"). Kord was the professor, more than a match, intellectually, for anyone in the management. Almost a teetotaler, of only average height, far from a fighter, he yet had an imperturbable self-possession, exhibiting great courage and confidence which in the present situation seemed, to Simpkins, Galinsky, Stubb, and Smith, totally unwarranted by the facts. Shannon was the "trickster," exuberant, mischievous, daring, and courageous; unlike an ordinary mortal, he seemed to possess an immunity from the consequences of flirting with disaster. Then the giant, Harold Lewis, silent, immense, powerful, and utterly fearless, had shouted his defiance to J. A. Bergson. The three of them must have loomed large in the sight of these four workers.

The decision to act was made. Kord and Shannon got word to front-welding, and before the end of the day Zyznomyrsky and Jaskiewicz in the press departments were informed: the demonstration was on.

The next morning before the beginning of the shift "there was a good deal of excitement and suspense." "Some of us waited [outside the plant] until all the members showed up, and verified that everybody was wearing his button." They went inside in groups. "Right up front Vasdekis, King Kong, Bill Lewis, William Cooper, Leonard Pinkowicz, and a couple of others [Sawdust and Alice the Goon among them] were ready to receive us—all wearing buttons." As they walked down the long aisle "front-welding, departments 18, 17, and 19, [and] even inspection was observing. They [had] not yet [begun] working; they were waiting along the aisles. There were some yells, cheering, yells, 'You show em!' More yells. Mostly what I saw was a festive occasion. There were small laughing groups. Mostly it was the second generation in evidence, some others were by their machines watching, not disinterested."

## Psychological Warfare

The commotion that followed lasted for days. In the hours after the morning demonstration a number of people came up to the union activists and asked for buttons. John Novak, the Slovak machinist, and the two other unionists in the toolroom were wearing buttons now, and buttons sprouted in the press departments. Again, as in the aftermath of the Lewis incident and the five-cent raise, a burst of activity erupted. "Our leaders in all departments were contacting workers on the job or at lunch."

By this time, the phenomenon of group joinings was a thing of the past. Membership gains occurred through the adherence of individuals to the union, although often members of a group would join close together. The influx of members in the press departments was greater now than it had been following the five-cent raise. Perhaps 55 percent of the workers in departments 17 and 19 were union members, up from about 25 or 30 percent following the five-cent raise. The strength of the union in front-welding moved to about 75 percent; in department 18 the union enjoyed the support of about 35 percent of the workers; in transportation union strength jumped to about 30 percent; in shipping to about 20 percent. Only three workers from the toolroom were union members, and inspection remained foreign territory. These membership gains began immediately after the demonstration, continued at a high level for several days, and then tapered off. Kord estimates that perhaps 50 percent of the membership was acquired in these brief periods following a dramatic breakthrough, and the influx which now followed was by far the largest.

These new members consisted mostly of second-generation Poles, and again among the press operators a subtle pattern was apparent. "The earlier hires were quicker on joining, the new hires were equally quick on wearing buttons." The former, Kord recalls, "were the best joiners," following whom "came the new hires and finally a scattering of first-generation Poles, Appalachians, and northern native Americans." In addition, Kord noticed that the earlier hires had a different, more rational, goal-oriented understanding of the union and that "they were a bit more serious about" it. On the other hand, "the new hires were having a ball to which they bought no tickets; and maybe they were joining a new type of gang as they saw it, a gang to which they wanted to belong."

The first generation remained generally uncommitted and fearful. In department 16, for example, the union hardly grew at all. Only Nick Buglaj and one or two second-generation Poles were union supporters. An incident in the button demonstration gives a sharp illustration of these attitudes of fearfulness that were so prevalent among the first generation. During the march through the aisle the second-generation workers had left their machines and gathered in small groups, laughing and cheering, and even the non-union workers in the inspection department had stopped to watch. Yet, in spite of their location along the line of march, the first-generation workers in department 16 had remained at their machines, quiet and undemonstrative. Nevertheless, although the first generation still remained apart from the union, "they all talked about the demonstration, a few here and there joining, but mostly not wearing buttons yet. But many of them showed sympathy, individually talking to some of us."

The button victory boosted the morale of the union and further confused and demoralized the company. The workers in torch-welding continued wearing buttons. It was heroic, yet easy, and they were gaining confidence. Ferment was intense among the new members in the press departments, the first generation was increasingly coming to believe in the ability and strength of the union, and even some of the workers in inspection seemed to Kord to respond more positively to the union. And the pre-Lewis militants were eager to take on the company.

The whole union was on the verge of some kind of eruption. Incidental group discussions sprang up; Sharkey's Bar became a center of agitation and fraternity, with frequent meetings in the back room. The unionists were volatile and aggressive. Their discussions were heated; the company was repeatedly denounced, excoriated, and mocked. Even the first generation was to some extent infected by this spirit. Although still outside the union, they began to hold discussions, mostly but not entirely among themselves, emerging from the shell of fear and submissiveness that seemed both to characterize them and to distinguish them from all other groups in the shop.

Kord, Shannon, Vasdekis, Pinkowicz, and several others were moving quite freely around the shop, talking to other workers.

The button victory opened this up beautifully. It created enthusiasm among the active [unionists, and] it gave courage. It seemed to cow management and gave us the appearance of large numbers. We were sending people to inspection, shipping, toolroom, and we seemed to have all the other departments in hand—even where we did not have majorities. We seemed to be the ones with the better ideas.

People now were willing to take time off from production. The cans became very popular discussion and agitation places. Of course production suffered, but not disastrously. We didn't want to force the company to act when they were so nicely immobilized.

There was a lot of visiting—in the departments and cans. I went to other departments many times a day—16, 17, 19, cans and inspection and shipping. Sixteen, 17, and 19 were receptive or better. The cans were very good. Other activists also came to us and [to the] front welders for planning and with information.

Altogether dozens of people were moving around the shop. Some would spend as many as ten to fifteen minutes away from their stations. The frequency increased to about three visits per day for each of these many "migrant" workers. They "were feeling pretty sure of themselves. They wanted to get around and kind of brag about things and show how confident they were."

When knots of men would form and discussions arise, the foremen might respond with a half-hearted "Break it up, fellas!" But in the several days following the demonstration they kept largely to the sidelines. And since the Lewis incident J. A. Bergson himself "was strangely inconspicuous in the plant."

A select group of leaders had been meeting frequently in the back room of Sharkey's. Kord, Shannon, Vasdekis, and Pinkowicz were usually present, but Robertson, the president, never attended these informal gatherings, and apart from his verbal militancy, he had never seemed very active. At any event, he did not frequent the bar—in the eyes of the front welders this was just as well. Robertson continued to arouse their suspicions. In this setting the leadership began to make its plans for the coming battle.

In the several days following the button demonstration the union had made what seemed clearly to be the last possible gains. "We couldn't go on forever getting new members. . . . The button push [had been] meant primarily to get us over the top—it didn't quite do that. . . . We were running out of happenings, and [the contract] was the happening most needed. To try for a contract was the next logical step." At one of these meetings—all of this took place around early June—Shannon, Kord, and Vasdekis "decided that [they] would have to enter into negotiations, bluff, and if worst came to worst, go for broke." "We were finding it tough going, we had reached the limits of this early growth and we had to move further." A few new members had trickled in after the upsurge following the button victory, but Kord, Shannon, Vasdekis, and Pinkowicz had by now become painfully aware of the obstacles to further organization.

About 25 percent of the work force were first-generation Poles; another 10 percent were first-generation Ukrainians. With a few exceptions they remained apart from the union.[1] About 10 percent of the workers were Appalachian migrants, a large number of whom seemed to be inside truck drivers (forklift, etc.). Feeling intensely alien in the midst of the mass of Slavic workers and scattered throughout the shop (rather than concentrated in a department, as the Ukrainians were in department 16), the Appalachians were "the most lonely and isolated people in the plant." With few exceptions they too remained apart from the union.[2]

The northern native Americans—most of whom were skilled—remained aloof or hostile. A large majority of the workers in the toolroom were of this background. They were "largely older . . . non-Catholic, conservative, better off, [enjoyed] greater security . . . some [were of] German extraction, [and] there were some Scandinavians." They were in their forties on the average, although a few were older. The three unionists in the toolroom, however, did not fit this general description. Luebke was "a bit younger than most"—apart from the fact that Kord had described him as somewhat "odd," Novak was a Slovak Communist, and within a week it would become clear what Robertson was.

The maintenance workers were likewise generally of northern native American or north European Protestant background, as were the setup men in departments 18, 16, 17, and 19. A strong majority of the workers in the inspection department were also of this extraction. These men had no common interests or associations with the Slavic and Lithuanian workers in the union, and they lived, not in Hamtramck, but in other parts of Detroit, quite a few of them on the west side.

On the other hand the first-generation immigrants were truly a part of the Hamtramck community. It is important to recall, however, that the peasant immigrants with whom we are now concerned had not undergone the transformative experiences of the second generation, and they continued to respond to social situations such as the present one (where the key question centered around a challenge to constituted authority) with much the same attitude as that which characterized the peasant community in the old country.[3] Such attitudes of fear and submissiveness—which should not be misconstrued as approval of the authorities—we have seen manifested on several occasions in the course of the union struggle. It is the persistence of the peasant culture in this case which I think accounts for the specific behavior of the first generation.

Yet additional factors served to further weaken the union. Not only did the shipping department, for example, lack a strong leader, but its location between the two most anti-union departments in the shop—the toolroom and inspection—isolated it from the influence of the unionists in the other departments and simultaneously brought the workers in this department under a variety of pressures, among them the aggressive anti-union activity of Al Schein. Union support in shipping was limited to the three blacks, Frenchy, and perhaps one or two second-generation Poles. Although the toolroom had three union members, one of them, President Robertson, was strangely inactive, while Luebke was "odd," and Novak, although helpful in working on the first generation, spoke broken English and was not an aggressive leader. One of the consequences of the removal of the early (1933) group of unionists from the toolroom was now apparent. This complex of circumstances resulted in a relatively weak union nucleus in the toolroom and in the isolation of the shipping department.

In the inspection department neither the higher rate of pay nor the greater status—the skill required was well below that of a toolmaker, but the status in the plant was more on a par with the latter--can account for the failure of the union to establish an outpost in this department. In all probability inspection would never have become a stronghold of unionism; on the other hand, there were a number of second-generation Poles in inspection who were sympathetic. Why then did the union fail to gain even a single member here?

Schein was the dominant personality in his department, and he was strongly opposed to the union. He was outspoken and aggressive, and it was known around the shop that he had the ear of the company and associated closely with the foremen. Strong circumstantial evidence led Kord and the others to suspect that he had been the informer on the committee which in 1933 had negotiated a wage increase. He was a Mason; all the foremen were Masons. He had been promoted to floor inspector; all the other members of the committee had been fired. The evidence might not have held up in court, but it led Kord and others to draw strong conclusions. As a floor inspector Schein had the complete freedom of the shop. "He went out to other departments doing miking, gauging, and spot checking; he was in touch, he could hear what was going on in 17, 19, cutoff, swagers, everyplace." He went to the shipping department and the toolroom, although he had no work-connected reason for doing so. He would go around the plant two or three times a day. When the union got started it seemed to Kord that he was listening to see what was happening and reporting what he heard. He did not go into the two welding departments, but he seemed to spend a lot of time with first-generation people and setup men. Kord surmises that he "warned" them of what would happen if they joined a union. He never made an explicit threat, but his presence and activity were psychologically intimidating.

Schein's main impact, though, was in his own department. Kord thinks that he definitely held back a number of workers in inspection from joining the union. We have already seen, in the case of torch-welding, what influence two strong personalities can have on the weaker workers in a department. In inspection, however, there were no strong pro-union personalities—no one, for example, of the caliber of such solid secondary leaders as Jaskiewicz and Zyznomyrsky. Even so, it might have taken a Kord or a Shannon merely to neutralize the influence of Al Schein. In a department where, in the absence of Schein the union might have gained at least a foothold, it achieved nothing. Without such a foothold, contact with the shipping department was limited to the messages that Wilson might bring in the course of his work. Such were the strategic circumstances which Kord perceived.

### Negotiations: The Choreography of Power

About a week after the button demonstration—probably the second week in June—the formal decision to enter into negotiations was made at a union meeting. The whole union was enthusiastically in favor of this course, yet only Vasdekis knew that the real strength of the union was far below its purported strength. Had the truth been known, it would have taken some of the steam out of the rank and file and simultaneously stiffened the company's resistance.

Robertson, the president of the local, was remarkably deficient in militancy. He had "confined his leadership to meetings [and had] talked well enough to sell himself, but he was not lending himself to vital things. He preferred to play for time and [he] advised caution all along. Some of us thought [that] time we didn't have too much of, we had to move, move, move."

Morris Field gave the best lead in formulating contract demands, but Kord also raised a number of points both in small gatherings and at meetings. "Overall the demands were modest but elemental": a steward on each shift in each department; a chief steward on each shift; a permanent grievance-handling committee for the final step of grievance procedure; seniority (at least departmental); call-in pay; an increase of the basic wage rate to a dollar an hour; and sole bargaining agency status for the union. At this time—and throughout the negotiations—the union continued to carry out its plans without the benefit of formal shop-floor organization. Only after the contract did stewards emerge. Meanwhile the unionists operated on the basis of the informal leadership structures that had developed spontaneously: Vasdekis and Pinkowicz in front, Kord and Shannon in torch, Jaskiewicz and Zyznomyrsky in the press departments, Zero in cutoff, Buglaj in swaging, and Wilson in transportation. Lew Thompson in shipping was beginning to emerge as a leader in his department, and of course, Luebke, Novak, and the problematical Robertson in the toolroom. The two centers of union strength—torch- and front-welding—continued to exercise informal leadership throughout the plant. Vasdekis and Pinkowicz were in touch with cutoff and departments 17 and 19. Kord and Shannon were in communication with swaging, 17, 19, and shipping, and during the later stages of negotiations they would establish tentative contact with inspection.

The negotiations got under way immediately. The atmosphere was charged: while the negotiators talked upstairs in J. A. Bergson's office, the unionists on the shop floor were breaking loose.

The negotiating committee, which included Vasdekis, Pinkowicz, Shannon, Luebke, and Robertson (there may have been one more committeeman), asked to meet with the management, in this case J. A. Bergson and his brother Walter. Although J. A. readily agreed to meet with the committee, "he was adamant at first in refusing to bargain because he didn't believe we represented a majority." Vasdekis and Shannon replied that he would just have to take their word for it or find out the hard way. "If you don't believe we represent a majority we can show you we do—we can strike the plant!"

As this first session developed, President Robertson appeared to be playing a peculiar role. "Be reasonable, fellas," he would say. "You can't go that far!" It seemed he would accept anything if he could get the others to go along. The union was asking for a minimum of over a dollar an hour (it was presently forty-five cents); Robertson was willing to settle for sixty cents. On the issues of grievance procedure, representation, and seniority, he seemed spineless and capitulating. The others on the committee quickly grew angry and suspicious. Johnny Ringwald (the representative from the UAW's regional office in Hamtramck), who was sitting in on the negotiations, also thought Robertson's behavior peculiar. Shannon and Vasdekis, responding to this threat, began to take over negotiations. Vasdekis was hard and relatively controlled; Shannon was angry and volatile. Pinkowicz and Luebke "were moderate by nature," but they supported the two militants, and the union had a divided negotiating committee.

The committee met every day with the Bergsons from nine-thirty in the morning to about two o'clock in the afternoon. Yet during the first week of negotiations J. A. Bergson refused to "accept the right of the union to talk for a majority." It was time to put on the floor show.

The breakdown of authority that had become "considerably" intensified after the five-cent raise and that had grown even more rapidly after the button demonstration now became explosive, proving to be the main ingredient in the company's fear of the union.

That's the way it was and that's the way we wanted it. This [turmoil] kept building up all through negotiations. I'm sure the company was getting reports on this development and its intensity during negotiations. With the elected officers in the negotiating room, it could easily appear as if things could just boil over.

I'm sure production suffered further. People would get together in groups to speculate about what was going on. [During the day] Shannon would get some gem of news to us, usually stirring things up a bit. "They don't believe we have a majority," he might say. "How can we convince them?" Sometimes a committeeman would go to the can in front and drop a few words that would galvanize a group of workers. They would spread it throughout the shop. These were shock waves. The committee was due to come down before three in the afternoon. By two or two-thirty people would stand in knots waiting for them in all departments. It would take Shannon a half hour to get to his own department.

Each day the committee came down there would virtually be a stoppage in the better-organized departments and the shock waves would carry us over to the next day. The committee was not giving complete reports and was letting imaginations work.

We were taking [our] cues from [the] committee and stirring things up in proper proportions. I got around a lot and a lot of people came to see me. Buttons were increasing, [and] some of us started wearing union caps made by unemployed garment workers at thirty-five cents each. We decorated the caps with buttons, and signs started appearing on walls, UAW slogans, headlines about strikes, etc.

As the negotiations continued into the second week the days became tense. People waited for progress reports, and when these were not forthcoming because there was no progress to report, small demonstrations of strength erupted on the shop floor. The more active people told the foremen that the company had better come across or else. People gathered more frequently and in greater numbers, discussing the situation. Their mood became more insubordinate, more aggressive. Some of these demonstrations "were planned, but the spontaneous ones, probably on cue, were very convincing. Mostly the negotiations were discussed—'will they or won't they?' Some foremen made feeble attempts to break it up—not all. Mostly the guys would slowly disperse and gather a bit later in different combinations and places." "Those departments that had one or two shifts had thirty-minute lunch breaks on their own time. They would visit and interfere with production elsewhere. [They] would stand around and talk for ten or fifteen minutes."

In these several days during which negotiations were stuck Kord "encouraged a crescendo" of this activity. On the other hand, some of the "hotheads and secondary leaders" were going beyond insubordination and making threats to the foremen. Kord discouraged this. Both he and Vasdekis tried to keep these unionists "within useful bounds." "We didn't want to provoke [the foremen] unnecessarily because they were relatively passive." And the foremen themselves "seemed confused, leaderless, and demoralized."

"There was very close coordination between the shows of strength in the plant and the tactics in negotiations used by Vasdekis and Shannon." The activity of Robertson had compelled Vasdekis and Shannon to take a strong stand, committing the union to a strike in the event they were completely rebuffed by Bergson. Yet they alone knew how weak the union really was. The situation was all too clear. "We were bluffing," recalls Kord. "We couldn't possibly have had a strike. If we had called a strike then we would have been clobbered once and for all. There is no question: if we [hadn't won] this bluff there would [have been] no second chance."[4] In essence a successful bluff was supposed to inspire another influx of members. Vasdekis, Shannon, Kord, and Pinkowicz expected not to gain a contract through majority representation, but rather to gain a majority through a contract.

Fortunately, Robertson knew nothing about the real strength of the union. During negotiations Vasdekis had confided in Shannon, and he had told Kord. In this war of nerves Robertson's role was paradoxical. Because he was taken in by the falsification of the union's strength he may have unwittingly aided Vasdekis and Shannon in maintaining Bergson's illusions on this score. On the other hand, Kord asks, "What good is it to have a divided committee? This could demoralize the other negotiators and undercut the position of the union."

Toward the middle of the second week Bergson, who so far had only a memory of defeat and humiliation at the hands of the union and who by this time must have lost all faith in Hamtramck's forces of "law and order," finally crumbled "under the impact of the turmoil downstairs and probably became convinced that we did have a majority." The discussions had so far been fruitless; now, however, Bergson "suddenly agreed to bargain . . . but bargaining lasted three or four days."

Once bargaining started things cooled down in the shop. Again on cue from the committee we started banking the fires. The foremen were noticeably relieved. Some even started fraternizing. Things got downright congenial in some spots, but some of the visiting continued, and some groups were visible but not blatant. In deference we used the cans more. Now even some of the inspectors started coming around to see us and ask for news. The gang was always waiting up front at two o'clock.

During these last few sessions "we were de-escalating generally, [but] if a stumbling block was struck, we would give another turn." Essentially, though, they had scored their victory when Bergson had begun to negotiate on the terms of a contract. If he "hadn't agreed to [such] negotiations we would have had to strike or see our union disappear." To Kord the outcome of such a stike was doubtful.

One day a triumphant committee came down about one-thirty and announced [that] they had reached an agreement. The committee was the center of attention; a crowd gathered around it in the front of the shop. The story spread like wildfire. The committee had to repeat it many times as new people came up to hear for themselves. There was jubilation, cheers, lots of movement, [people moving around] spreading the word. Our next batch of members started becoming evident. People we had talked to fruitlessly before started being friendly. A new shift was in the making.

The members of the committee, Kord, and the secondary leadership (Jaskiewicz, Zyznomyrsky, Zero, Buglaj, and Wilson) went to the back room of Sharkey's to figure out how to get the majority they had claimed to already have, and to do other planning. They had achieved an impressive victory, but they knew that they had only won the battle, not the war. There were serious weaknesses in the contract. Through the activity of Robertson they had gotten only two hours of call-in pay, and even worse they had only gotten classification seniority within a department.[5] The seventy-five cent minimum was, under the circumstances, relatively insignificant. And, like all other auto unions at the time, they had gotten recognition for members only. Two years of serious struggle lay ahead; and with a president who seemed to be an agent of the company the union was immediately confronted with a crisis in leadership.

# CHAPTER FOUR

# Expansion

IN THE SEVERAL WEEKS following the contract the union expanded rapidly. The leadership engaged immediately in confrontations with Schein and Robertson. The successful, decisive outcome of these confrontations established the union and particularly the authority of the leadership on a higher level. In the center of the shop the second-generation militants acquired more than a taste for power. For over a year, beginning soon after the contract, they engaged in an uninterrupted series of shop-floor activities which took the form of slowdowns and wildcats. Out of all this emerged a definite, although low-key, political system of alliances and relationships as the union leadership sought to incorporate the entire shop under its jurisdiction. Within this system, hitherto submerged differences of culture and personality became more articulate. In many ways the political life within the plant was a microcosm reflecting similar processes endemic to the broader society of which the union was a part.

## Rapid Growth

Like the other events, the success of the union in compelling the company to yield on the question of the contract resulted in a large influx of new members. Nevertheless, this growth was not general, but proceeded along ethnocultural and political lines. In the transportation department the hand-truck operators, most of whom were first-generation Poles, were now drawn into the union. About 60 percent of them became members, compared with about 75 percent of the power-truck operators, most of whom were more militant second-generation Poles. They had in fact started joining the union much earlier, some as early as the time of the five-cent raise. Here Elmer Wilson would develop into a leader of considerable ability. The toolroom workers remained unresponsive. Kord thinks that the "ethnic makeup" of the department and "a certain feeling of superiority" were "great deterrents" to organization. Throughout the plant the Appalachians were also relatively slow to join.

Why the first-generation workers were more responsive than the non-Slavic workers is not exactly clear. Although practically all of the first-generation helpers in front-welding joined the union after the contract and its ratification, only about 60 percent of the first-generation swagers and press operators were members at the same time. The great strength of the union among the first-generation helpers in the front-welding department must therefore be attributed to the character of the union in that department. Not only were two of the leaders of the union, Vasdekis and Pinkowicz, the key people in the department, but there was also a solid cadre of secondary leadership (Lewis, Cooper, and King Kong) and a number of strong union men among the second generation. In contrast, only Nick Buglaj played any leadership role among the swagers in department 16, and his activity was not very forceful. In the press departments there was more militancy. Frank Jaskiewicz and Johnny Zyznomyrsky were good, aggressive secondary leaders, but the character of the union in these departments was still quite distinct from that of the front-welding department. As we shall see later, the young workers in the press departments (especially in department 19, where the new hires were concentrated) were rather anarchic and spontaneous; the union here was less structured, more an extension of the gang spirit of the neighborhood. On the other hand, the discipline and solidity of the union cadres in the front-welding department presented an entirely different set of circumstances to the first-generation helpers. In a word, the union possessed a more authoritative presence. And as we shall see, each department developed its own special character. To the extent that the union's presence in a department is both solid and forceful, it can compel assimilation. There was no intimidation as such, but the coherence, discipline, and forceful character of the union—the persistent but not hostile efforts of the militants to recruit the remaining first generation—must be construed as a kind of pressure. That the first-generation workers were sympathetic is not denied; but the process of joining involved something other than mere sympathy.

The leading position of Pinkowicz must also have aided in the recruitment of the first generation in the front-welding department. Pinkowicz had a certain standing among the Catholic and more moderate workers in the plant. He was a moderating influence on Vasdekis, who in turn was able to control the more volatile King Kong, Cooper, Lewis, and Alice the Goon. Thus, both the discipline and self-control of the union in this department and the presence of Pinkowicz in a position of influence must have encouraged the first-generation workers in front-welding to throw in their lot with the union earlier than those in other departments.

It should be noted that mere membership figures are an inadequate means by which to gauge the strength of the union. Although the momentum was on the side of the organizers, and while from the standpoint of historical hindsight we might be led to conclude that the success of the union was a foregone conclusion, the future did not seem so patently assured to these early unionists. The new members—particularly the first generation—were indecisive and subject to various pressures; among them was a periphery that could conceivably melt away if the union suffered any setbacks before it achieved further growth and organizational consolidation. And the native Americans, the toolroom workers, a number of inspectors led by Schein, the maintenance men, and the setup men remained hostile. It was a situation filled with dangers. The crisis in leadership had not only to be resolved, but it had to be worked out in such a way as to most effectively take advantage of the strategic situation.

### The Bert Robertson Affair

The strange behavior of Robertson during the contract negotiations had become known to a number of the more active unionists. One of the union militants, either under direction from the leadership or on his own initiative, had trailed Robertson to Bergson's residence. The evidence was sufficient: Robertson was working for the company. This was not seen directly as a threat. The militant members of the union were feeling pretty confident now; "they were all ready for a bit of red meat after they had worked so hard and arrived." But how to deal with Robertson? The crisis over him was felt mostly within the ranks of the primary and secondary leadership. There were a number of gut ideas ("throw him out of the shop," "let King Kong handle him") but no thought-out idea, no reckoning with the strategic political and psychological situation within the plant. It was during this event that Kord's particular abilities came to the fore: in the crisis of leadership, Kord took the initiative.

The members of the committee responded in a more balanced way than the militants: they knew that something had to be done, and they sought to bring Kord into the decision-making. They were inclined to go for a trial procedure. Kord thought that they could avoid that and should if possible. He did not think that it would be good at this point; "we still needed to weld an organization." Others were also a bit uncertain about the possible consequences of a trial. Kord felt that they "could still go that route if other things failed, and they would have time to prepare the ground better." He suggested instead that they force Robertson to resign the presidency. A trial would only have taken much of the initiative from the union, given Robertson (and implicitly the company) a platform, and allowed Schein, Bergson, the foremen, and the anti-union workers an opportunity to coalesce. It would also have subjected the relatively weak first generation to strong countervailing pressures. The basis for the union's strength among them was the fact that the union cadres and leadership had exercised the prerogatives of authority. They had been on the move since the Lewis incident, they had expanded the range and intensity of their activity during and following the button victory, and they had finally taken command of the situation during the contract negotiations. In dealing with Robertson, Kord thought, the union should maintain its aggressive and decisive character. He agreed to draft a resignation letter and present it to Robertson.

The next day we [Kord and Shannon] waited for Robertson to come down the aisle from the toolroom, down the aisle between stock and press, then down the aisle between torch and press to near the can where he would be working on a press die. We waited a couple of minutes until he started the job, then went up to him. I did the brief talking, gave him a copy of the letter and told him we expected his signature within twenty-four hours. His reputation was already shot in this part of the shop. The guys nearby moved slightly away but not far enough to miss much and kept glancing in our direction with smirks. Shannon had a tight smile that could easily fade if need be. When I revealed the gist of the problem Robertson turned white, then ashen, like his cigar ash. He listened, denied nothing, read the letter, and asked, "What if I don't?" I followed with a remark like, "You will or else!" and we walked away. Robertson was a lost soul for a couple of minutes, left the job unfinished and went back to the toolroom. We didn't see him again until the next morning. We were waiting near the aisle. When he walked by on the way to the toolroom he stopped just long enought to hand me the letter without a single word and left. Needless to say, I felt relief.

The young second-generation workers began to unleash their hostility. But Kord and the rest of the leadership, concerned to spare Robertson any further embarrassment, passed the word to leave him alone and not to rub it in. Kord explained his thinking as follows: the fact that Robertson had surrendered was in itself a forceful expression of the strength of the union. Also, Kord "never seemed to be comfortable with *unnecessary* infliction of pain. If the situation had required it I could have gone further, but Robertson was now immobilized and harmless. Furthermore, if they had pressed him after that the reaction among some of the reluctants might have been bad. Remember, we still had the job of recruitment to do." The leadership tried to prevent a "bullfight atmosphere." Some of the people who had joined reluctantly and many of those not yet in "would probably have reacted negatively to an overkill." Robertson, although he remained a member of the union, quickly faded from view. His presence, Kord thought, was living proof of the strength of the union.

In contrast to some of the more volatile suggestions, like "let King Kong get him," this strategy of Kord's must seem moderate. Surely it would have been an easy matter to get rid of Robertson. Yet the object was not simply to eliminate him. Rather, the logic of the situation demanded that the union use this confrontation in such a way as to further enhance its authoritative character. Remember, few people outside the primary and secondary leadership knew what was going on before the resignation; and how much more effective must it have been to retain Robertson as an empty shell and a living example of the strength of the union? To have thrown him out or beaten him up could easily have been the work of one or two; to keep him around would demonstrate the power of the union.

The validity of this tactic became clear in the immediate aftermath. The forced resignation was an "event"; perhaps an additional 10 percent of the workers joined the union. Among the first generation the impact was somewhat greater: about 15 percent of them entered the union. Again, the ability of the union to assert its dominance through its handling of Robertson was an important factor in reassuring the first generation and convincing them that the union, not the company, controlled the situation and could guarantee their security.

### The Al Schein Affair

The Robertson episode had a more dramatic impact in the inspection department. Al Schein could no longer hold back everybody in inspection. A couple of inspectors had joined after the contract, and a few more did so after the Robertson affair. As Kord saw it, following the contract a group of inspectors was emerging that would clearly join the union. Shannon and Kord had talked to a few, and "they weren't too reluctant to talk." These inspectors had more frequent contacts with the rank-and-file second-generation workers in the press departments and, with the exception of one Hungarian, were second-generation Poles. The union had thus established a wedge in this department, and the general increase of membership following the contract and the forced resignation of Robertson, as well as the psychological impact of the latter episode on relations of authority and on the morale of the anti-union forces, led Al Schein to conclude that the greater part of wisdom consisted in joining with the union forces. The same week that Robertson resigned Schein came up to either Kord or Shannon or both and asked for some applications. He came back the same day with half a dozen new members, "mostly people we couldn't yet touch." (Schein had always had a certain leadership quality among a particular type— those less than totally committed to the union. He even became steward during the war period. Yet overall a *modus vivendi* was developed and maintained between Schein and the union.) The group that Schein brought into the union consisted generally of non-Slavs. Noticeable among them was a group of four Scotsmen and a third-generation German. The exception to this generalization was a second-generation Russian who was a Mason. (He was never a good union man and was probably an informer. When he became foreman the union gave phony information to the company by letting him overhear "conversations.")

If in return for this act of "goodwill" Al Schein thought that the union leaders would be grateful, or at least accommodating, he quickly found out otherwise. Kord, sensitive to the real psychological relationships of power and authority that had prevailed in the plant, had been waiting for this moment. Schein was the kingpin of an informal network of anti-union people in the plant. In addition to his Masonic ties both to other workers and to the foremen, he was in contact with and influential among the setup men, who "were much closer to him in mentality and allegiance." In addition, while the first-generation workers had never really been followers of Schein, his presence and activity among them constituted a heavy countervailing force to that of the union. Thus, perhaps after the contract, and certainly after the Robertson resignation, Kord suggested the tactic of bringing Schein to trial as soon as he joined the union.

This idea was primarily Kord's, "Some union militants would have preferred to resort to rough stuff at some point." But after the breakthrough in inspection following the contract and the Robertson affair, the union leaders were confident that Schein would soon join, not out of conviction, but out of opportunism and necessity. After some discussion Kord was able to convince the top leadership of the wisdom of this strategy. As Kord remembers: "There wasn't too much difficulty in selling the idea. It seemed to offer a way of continuing the membership drive and would not have too adverse a reaction on some of the more difficult prospects. Following this, the top leadership sold the idea to the secondary leadership, which was pretty well disciplined."

Events followed quickly. A special meeting was called at which formal charges were presented. The offense was "conduct unbecoming a union member," and the charges were roughly that Schein "was early discouraging the idea of unionism, that he was spreading fear, that he held back inspection effectively as long as he could, and joined only after he saw he had a lost cause; that he proved his influence when he brought in a group." At the next regular meeting a special trial committee of seven or nine members was elected, and charges were delivered by registered mail. It was probably the second Sunday in August that the trial meeting was held. Although the session was not general, it was opened to all parties concerned and was heavily attended: it was an *event.* Vasdekis was the prosecutor; Schein denied everything. There was never any doubt about the outcome, however. By a unanimous vote the jury found him guilty and ordered him to pay a fine of fifty dollars—a lot of money in those days.

The problem was, would he pay it? Now that the union had committed itself to a showdown, it had to be prepared to enforce its ruling. At the time of the verdict it was not clear whether Schein would pay, in which case the union would have had to carry the struggle one step further, probably to the point of stationing some of the tough guys at the gate to keep Schein from entering. It was a showdown they wanted to avoid. Thinking it wise to leave the matter hanging for twenty-four hours, the leadership did not press the matter on the day of the trial, and afterwards Schein never told anyone that he would not pay. But the next day,

we approached him in the shop and asked him how he wanted to pay. He said he didn't have that much money. We told him he could pay five dollars down and the rest within three months. He paid the five dollars that day and we were pretty sure he would pay the rest. There was a visible sigh of relief [on the part of Kord and the others]. It seemed clear who had won. The capitulation had a greater effect than the trial itself. If there had been some feeling of apprehension over the trial, the capitulation dispersed that.

In terms of further recruitment, the impact of the Schein capitulation was mixed. Slow, steady gains continued to be made among the first generation, although as a result of Schein's capitulation these were sped up somewhat. The toolroom, which Kord considered "our greatest challenge and sore spot," yielded a couple of new members, but the setup men were not happy with the outcome and the union made no further gains among them.

On the other hand, in the inspection department the pace of recruitment quickened. Al Schein had lost some of his following as a result of his capitulation, although he was never rendered totally ineffectual. His role was not shattered, but it was greatly diminished—"It was good enough for us," Kord remembers. Some of the other anti-union workers would have preferred to see Schein hold out, Kord thinks. But the department was already slipping out of his control and joining the union by the time of the trial. Of all the anti-union people Schein really showed the greatest leadership quality and had a definable following. But he was rather careful not to be too open about it. "That's why we thought he would bend. A number of his followers remained on the sidelines until they saw that the union could make its verdict stick. The remaining holdouts were fragmented. Some of them wanted some approach from a high level to be convinced and join with a face saver." As a result the union signed up a substantial majority of the inspectors shortly after Schein's capitulation.

## Leadership: The Emergence of Kord as President

When a handful of workers set out in early 1937 to build a union, the real structure, the concrete details, the problems and the responsibilities that would arise were not—and could not have been—foreseen. Beyond the idea of organizing all the workers in the shop for the purpose of collective bargaining, the concept of a union remained relatively vague.

In those first months before the contract, the union was at a primitive stage of its development. Its membership, confined almost exclusively to second-generation Polish production workers, faced the relatively simple (though risky) task of expansion. The main form of activity was propaganda—talking to other workers. Until the button victory the activities of the leadership (to a great extent the leadership and the union were indistinguishable at this time) were concerned with either routine functions like running meetings and collecting dues or the symbolic functions of being the visible embodiment of a union which was as yet hardly active. Shannon, Vasdekis, and Kord were talking union strongly to selected people, sounding out others, and generally taking more chances than the others. Pinkowicz was doing the same, but more cautiously. Bill Lewis and King Kong were making progress in their department, but were largely under Vasdekis' leadership; they had less understanding of the essence of unionism. Leo Ptasz did some cautious work in his own department, torch-welding. He never did develop into a leader, but the department knew he was a member, and that helped. Frank Jaskiewicz and Johnny Zyznomyrsky were breaking ground in the press departments and reaching out to each other's departments; they were significantly more active than Ptasz.

It was the kind of situation in which the requirements of leadership were simple and undifferentiated: Robertson's success at becoming president was therefore an indication of the naïveté of the early unionists (if they had had among them an experienced unionist he might have noticed the unreal and therefore suspicious character of Robertson's outspokenness). More significantly, however, that success was a reflection of the lack of a suitably differentiated and challenging objective situation in response to which qualities of leadership and personality could emerge. Prior to the negotiations, for example, Shannon occupied a position in the leadership hierarchy second only to Vasdekis. "He was a more picturesque guy" than Kord; "he was much more one of the boys; he always had an apropos quip, and he had obvious courage. He always had easier access to people and had a winning personality. He could rabble-rouse the plant in no time. Sometimes that was his assignment. He was an effective leader in some ways, but on a shallower level. He himself realized his limitations."

On the other hand, Kord was quiet, was not seeking a leadership position (even though he was one of the initiators of the organizing effort), and appeared a bit odd to some (he did not drink and was going to college). Kord ranked number three in this informal rating scheme (Pinkowicz was number four, Lewis number five). In spite of this, within his own department Kord was the major leader, and between himself and Shannon it was understood that Kord was the more capable unionist. Yet Shannon had charisma, and at this point the large role charisma played could stand as a summary expression not only of the character of early leadership, but of the sharp objective limitation on the range and depth of the union's practice in this embryonic stage. Such limitations were obvious in the character of the early confrontations. Until the button victory the union had remained relatively passive. The Lewis incident and the five-cent raise had been spontaneous responses to the aggression of the management and had occurred within the context of a general labor upsurge. In addition a pervasive sense of uncertainty and fear among the small parts companies in the Detroit area had led to a systematic overestimation of the power of the UAW. It was not until the button demonstration that the union took the initiative. And here it was Kord who provided the impulse, the strategic conceptualization and the tactical finesse. Yet the overall impact of the button demonstration, although it raised Kord's standing, did not change the 1–2–3 order. Within the top activist circles it was known that Kord was largely responsible for carrying out the demonstration, but only to a considerably lesser extent was this realized throughout the shop.

Not until after the contract, in his handling of the Robertson situation, did Kord come into prominence as a major leader. Although the discovery of a spy in the highest office of the union might seem to be crisis enough, as we have already noted this was a basic symptom of the historical weakness of the leadership in those early months. The crisis of leadership could have developed with Shannon as president (on the basis of our description of Robertson's ascension to the presidency, Shannon would have been the likely second choice). The point is, a time of testing faced the union in this critical period, and of necessity charisma yielded to organizational and political skill. At any rate, the Robertson affair gave Kord a big boost, and at this point, Kord surmises, it might have occurred to some people that he would be a good president. Shannon was obviously impressed. Kord thinks that he was the one who might have suggested such a move to the others. The last suspicions of the front welders dissipated: Vasdekis accepted Kord as in effect a coleader with Shannon and himself; Pinkowicz and Kord now got to know each other better; Bill Lewis now extended his approval to Kord; and Jaskiewicz and Zyznomyrsky came more definitely under Kord's influence.

The reaction among the active rank and file was "very positive." Kord became "a lot more known and a lot more popular. It was at this point that 'Professor' became common currency in the shop." Kord "very much felt like the man of the hour . . . there was a broad recognition of leadership in" him. The first generation and some inspectors "seemed to show a bit of awe, a hesitant out-reaching to me, signs of recognition and a willingness to come closer."

The nomination of Kord for president was a leadership affair. "The top leaders must have thought it out pretty well. I think they prepared the secondary leadership for it. I suspect the spadework was done pretty thoroughly because there was no second nomination. There was no sign of opposition." Meanwhile Shannon, the most popular and boisterous man in the union, was probably building up Kord's reputation in the other sections of the shop. In spite of this support, Kord's nomination depended less on his popularity with the rank and file than on the decision of the primary leadership. They initiated the decision, convinced Lewis, King Kong, Ptasz, Zyznomyrsky, Jaskiewicz, Zero, Alice the Goon, and Jake Stolz, and then "sold it more broadly to the membership." Thus, about a month after the ratification of the contract and two weeks after the resignation of Robertson, Kord was elected president.

Probably within a week of Kord's election Al Schein joined the union. The ensuing confrontation was the first test of Kord's leadership. The strategy decided on was seen as "primarily my thing, though I had full support. I had to make it work," Kord emphasizes. What distinguished Kord's approach to the problem from that of the others was his systematic conception of the union as a political-military organism. His application of force was not random violence (which he abhorred), but rather the disciplined use of political *power* (which implies a readiness to use force, but in a manner subordinated to an overall political strategy). The contrast between some of the young volatile second-generation workers (who were always ready for a fight) and Kord's calculating, self-disciplined intellectual approach is striking. The young militants were sometimes ready to throw a foreman over the fence; Kord aimed at establishing an organization that would alter the relationship of power in the plant. The Schein episode was an example of this subordination of tactics to strategy. Its success solidified Kord's position.

### Applying the Pressure: The Absorption of the Fringes

After the Schein trial it was clear that the union had won. Within a few weeks after the contract almost all of the Slavs had joined the union. With the breaking of the inspection department, the shipping department was brought within range of the union's influence, and the union very quickly entrenched itself. Within eight weeks of the Schein trial about 90 percent of the workers were union members. However, the last 10 percent of those were workers who only reluctantly and under great pressure had joined the union, and within eight months the other 10 percent were forced to submit. This group of 20 percent never really accepted the union and was thought to be a serious but manageable threat. The considerable energies of the militants now focused on removing this threat.

The group of more or less anti-union workers had one feature in common: they were non-Slavic Protestants. Among these were a number of Appalachians. Kord notes that, in contrast to the other holdouts, the Appalachians were moved by conviction, although some may have stayed out because they continued to court the company's favor. This moral character of the Appalachians was noticeable on the other side of the union fence as well. Those who joined the union did so out of conviction, and, in contrast to the first-generation workers and the gang subgroups among the second generation, the act of joining was highly individual. Those who held out took a lot of "convincing" and joined not because they were ultimately convinced that it was good, but rather "because the pressure started growing on them. More and more activists would talk to them, pressure them; and finally, if necessary, some of the big guys like King Kong and Alice the Goon would go over and 'talk to them.' " In this manner they were convinced.

There were a number of Scotsmen in the plant, particularly in the inspection department. None of these joined the union early. In the toolroom, the native Americans, Scandinavians, and Germans proved to be the biggest problem of all. Yet even here the union began to make some headway. There was a group of workers in the toolroom whose work required them to travel around the shop. They might have to make sure a die was working properly, or they might have to repair one. These workers were consequently more exposed to the psychological mood of the rest of the shop, they knew more people, they were more aware of the realities of the shop, and they also came under more pressure from the union militants because of greater contact with them. Whenever one of them had to check a die in one of the presses, some second-generation militant would work on him. Thus, these particular toolmakers got recruited into the union earlier than those whose work never required them to leave the back of the shop. These stationary workers were more isolated, ingrown, and stable. Because they formed such a solid milieu in the back of the shop, they were able to reinforce their negative attitudes toward the union, thus posing a special problem. One of the key gains made by the union, however, was greater mobility and increased contact among the workers. The union could thus make its presence more strongly felt than before the contract.

Vasdekis, Shannon, or once in a while King Kong would stroll down the shop. Shannon might say to King Kong, "Let's go back there and talk to somebody." These guys in the welders were always looking for something like that—they liked excitement. If they heard about somebody resisting joining, it was entirely within their psychology that King Kong and maybe Sawdust would go down there to visit. They would see this particular guy and joke around with him, but in such a way that he wasn't sure whether or not they were really only joking. Sometimes they would lean on a guy—"this bullshit's gotta stop—you know goddamn well you gotta join the union. You might as well do it soon." Mostly they wouldn't start this way—they would go in and put in their presence, leave an impression. This sort of thing wore them [the other workers] down.

The workers in the maintenance department were not as much trouble as those in the toolroom; they were not in a position to resist easily. The office, equipment, and lunch area of these workers was located in the middle of the shop between torch-welding and the press departments. Not only did they thus come under the direct influence of two of the most militant sections of the plant, but their work took them to other parts of the shop as well, where other militants could work on them.

The setup men were a difficult group, in part because of the corruption mentioned earlier. Often the big guys like Lewis or King Kong got the job of "convincing" them. Sometimes special groups were sent to "talk to them."

Obviously, the objective in recruiting these hostile workers was not to make them good union members, but to bring them under the jurisdiction of the union, wear them down, and scatter their potential for opposition. Once they were brought within the framework of the union, they were effectively beyond the reach of the management. Nevertheless, this strategy was politically necessary, and although successful it brought with it a peculiar set of problems. Twenty percent of the union consisted of worn-down members. Eighty percent of the toolroom were in this category, as well as 50 percent of inspection, most of the setup men, and some of the maintenance workers. These workers were resentful, and while they did nothing overt to undermine the union—they did not form caucuses and had no real political coherence—they revealed their attitudes in other ways.

Chief among these was resistance to the collection of dues. At this time there was no check-off; instead, the stewards were responsible for collecting dues. "Some guys who joined us felt they could refrain from paying dues. Those who had joined under pressure would often fall behind in their dues and not pay until the eighty-ninth day." (After ninety days the penalty was suspension; reinstatement depended on paying a fine.) The leadership had lists of these "eighty-niners": most would pay up shortly before suspension. None of them were Slavic. Instead, they numbered among themselves Appalachians, inspectors, die makers, and maintenance workers. As Kord saw it: "We had to police this. If a guy got suspended, we had to collect the fine, which was another showdown." (The fines were two dollars apiece; "the big guys were sent to collect them.") "Our job," Kord recalls, "was not only further recruiting, but to keep those we had from getting suspended. If they got suspended we had to collect the fine. Then, when we were able to prevent suspension after ninety days, we changed the rule to suspension after sixty days" (this took place within a year). Consequently, the eighty-niners now became fifty-niners. Falling behind in dues was obviously opposition to the union, and Kord's strategy consisted of removing this threat through controlling it. If the leadership had tried "to tighten up too soon they might have triggered something more serious. They had to use time to convince some of them."

Another group that posed problems were the "carpers," many of whom were found among the second generation. At least one of the Scots was a carper, as well as some of the Schein group. The carpers, however, were basically with the union; yet a certain kind of dissatisfaction came out in their carping. Some were carpers because they were not quite sold on the union; they felt they had no part in the decision-making process.

[As Kord explained it] the people who finally become leaders always create the impression, especially at the beginning, of being a clique. They have to be a little bit strong arm, a little bit secretive, and they've got to use strength where necessary. They create the impression of operating as a clique. That is the way it appears to people: they see a committee, they see some people close to the committee, and they get the idea that this is an organization to which they belong but which doesn't really respond to them. To a considerable degree their feelings are expressed as "ah, a clique runs this union. . . ."

The case of Walter Adams illustrates this problem. Adams was one of the biggest carpers. He was young, in his twenties, with a much greater degree of basic intelligence and a high school education. He was more open to ideas and eventually even joined the Socialist party. Because he was an inspector, however, he was isolated from the early activities of the unionists. For their part, the unionists maintained a distrust of the entire inspection department that only reinforced this isolation, even after they had gained a solid footing in it. Adams's isolation was broken down when Kord, in response to Adams's criticism of "cliquism," offered him a chance to undertake some responsibility. Adams accepted and was appointed to the safety committee—an important position in the plant, endowed with the authority to shut down malfunctioning machines. Adams's involvement with union activities steadily increased, and ultimately he became president of the local.

With the successful mopping-up operation the 10 percent of the work force that continued to hold out came under increasing pressure, and the union was confident that the holdouts would yield. With the crisis period past, a number of centrifugal tendencies—a kind of nonpolitical factionalism—broke the surface. The seniority system was completely inadequate and became the source of an unhealthful and sometimes explosive bickering. And minor but numerous wildcat strikes erupted.

# CHAPTER FIVE

# Factionalism

PERHAPS FACTIONALISM is too strong a word. No ideological or programmatic differences emerged in the seniority disputes or the wildcat strikes, and no opposing slates were fielded. The differences that appeared are more discernible to the historian than they were to the participants. They were rooted in culture, expressed in something that we might call a "mood" (being careful here to indicate that this term has an as yet undefined and imprecise, but definitely historical meaning), and in the last analysis amounted to a tendency possessing a low level of historical articulation.

## Disputes Over Seniority

That inequities existed in the seniority system was all too clear. Classification within a department meant that a man with one or two years of seniority might continue working while another with several years' seniority who was able to do the former's work would be laid off. It was a most unsatisfactory arrangement and the cause of much bitterness. The union leadership was determined to eliminate it, preferring in its stead shop-wide seniority. But for the first year the union was stuck with it.

At the ratification meeting the relief at getting a contract was so great and the lack of experience in relation to matters of seniority so complete, that together with the other aspects of the contract the implications of the seniority clauses were not fully understood. Nevertheless, some of the system's drawbacks were obvious. "People started looking for seniority systems that would be most advantageous to them individually and to their individual small group. . . . Even before we agreed to it, people discussed the seniority provisions. . . . Nobody was satisfied with it; we had to sell it on the basis that it was the first contract. . . . We wanted to broaden out" the seniority provisions in the contracts to follow. These disagreements were not serious enough to stop the contract, "because the contract overrode the whole thing, but you could already see the seeds of disagreement." Yet overall the discussion at the ratification meeting was fairly rational. The eruption of rampant individualism and the emergence of differing attitudes toward the problem would not occur until a major layoff.

The economy wasted little time in putting the local to the test. The late summer of 1937 saw a precipitous decline in industrial production, with the automobile industry especially hard hit. Chrysler, one of the Detroit Parts Company's important customers, cut its employment drastically. Commenting on this situation, R. J. Thomas, a regional UAW official, warned that "we may have to open negotiations with no employees in the shop."[1] The last quarter of 1937 was thus a time of severe testing for the young auto union.

As the workers in the Detroit Parts Company began to be hit by layoffs, the critical question was posed, Who gets sent home? And as the relationship between the seniority system and the business cycle in the automobile industry became clearer, each worker began demanding a seniority system that would best protect his position. "Everybody was asking the question individually and departmentally: What system was best for me and us?" This was interest-group politics at its worst. The department that had lots of work wanted departmental seniority; the department that was threatened wanted shop seniority, so that they could bump others with less seniority in other departments. Least worried were the highly skilled workers (and to a great extent this included the front welders as far as security was concerned); but when jobs were interchangeable, when a worker could easily learn another job in a couple of days, such questions came up as, "Why should I get laid off from this department when a guy with two days less seniority is still working in another department, and I could do his job?" When notified of a layoff the offended worker often rushed up to his departmental steward, the chief steward, a committeeman, or one of the officers and lodged this and similar complaints. The second-generation worker would be volatile and angry, the first-generation worker less vociferous; but both keenly felt the injustice of the situation. Such agitation around the plant spilled over into union meetings, where "there were some real hassles." People would jump up shouting and in the midst of general disorder the chairman would lose control.

In addition to the obvious centrifugal dangers inherent in the first seniority system, another more insidious problem existed. If, as happened regularly, the company was "putting on" a new job, it had some flexibility in deciding to which department that job would be assigned. Thus the door was opened to favoritism and dependence on the management. If one department was solidly union, for example, the company could put a new job in another where the workers were "better behaved" and give them the protection of having seniority in an expanding department. In this way the management would have been able to create groups of loyal workers who owed their jobs to managerial favoritism. Such a situation would obviously weaken the power of the union, for the whole question of the union's permanence and solidity hinged on winning the obedience and allegiance of that 50 percent of the work force (more or less according to circumstances) who were passive or even anti-union. The key to gaining this support lay in control of the job. Thus, from a strategic political standpoint alone the union had to wrest from the management the power of guaranteeing job security.

In varying degrees of intensity the seniority problem lasted for several years. "Literally, the whole plant was in turmoil, all the unskilled. We never had more turmoil than on these problems. It was a big battle, and at times it seemed dangerous. You fought this thing tooth and nail, but always within the organization. There was never a question of solidarity in the face of the company, but there was a lot of heat while you were debating, which carried over into the shop. Some local unions do break over this question. We didn't."

The response to inequities was refracted through the cultural and political structures in the plant. Torch-welding was hardest hit. It was a small department with several classifications in which most of the tasks were interchangeable. Yet in spite of the greater number of inequities, only Hillbilly, the youngest welder, caused any trouble. Here, Kord thinks, leadership was a factor; the presence of himself and Shannon, as well as of a well-knit band of union members, tended to prevent any outbreak. Likewise, the front-welding department also had its layoffs, yet there was no real problem there, probably in part for the same reason: the presence of a well-knit union infrastructure possessed of strong leadership. There was some trouble in department 18, but the real center of eruptions over the seniority system was in the press departments. Yet, looked at objectively, the inequities in these departments were less onerous than in some others. There were fewer classifications and more people, and to the press operators the system seemed to work more reasonably. The main cause of the furor was the earlier hires, who had greater length of service than the new hires and who therefore felt more aggrieved when hit by the inequities of the seniority system. Significantly, among the earlier hires it was the less active and the nonactive union men who were involved. The leading 25 percent of the earlier hires "would be more inclined to look toward a solution to the problem. . . . the guys who were not active to start with in any degree but just went along [were] interested first in how this would affect them . . . not the principle of the thing. They would try to finagle things so that they could stay and someone else get laid off."

Conflicts sometimes broke out between departments 17 and 19 (the workers in the former were older and had more seniority). When work was cut back in department 17 and not in 19, the men laid off complained that they could do the same job in 19. When a department was hard hit the steward spoke up for his men. Johnny Zyznomyrsky certainly did. Yet this opposition never rose beyond a primitive level of articulation. No one had any alternative program. The responses were *ad hoc:* each time the problem came up the injured party wanted things done differently. As the leadership saw it, however, the union was bound by the contract, and any revision of the seniority provisions could not be undertaken piecemeal, but had to be approached from an overall standpoint. The seniority squabbles continued to build to a certain level, but if nobody was laid off they would die down. The dissatisfaction erupted only when the problem did; it never got completely out of control, and there were no wildcats over this issue, only hard feelings.

## Wildcat Strikes

To a greater extent than the seniority squabbles, the wildcat strikes were centered primarily among the second-generation press operators, particularly in department 19.[2] The strikes were mainly over production standards, that is, the pace of work, although the issue of reclassification of wage rates for specific operations might also have cropped up. It must be understood at the outset, however, that these strikes—the word itself is misleading—were minor, low-key affairs, limited in extent and lacking in forcefulness, never posing a serious threat to the hegemony of the leadership cadre in the plant. Fewer than 10 percent of these actions involved as much as a whole department. More than 75 percent of them concerned a single operation, which might involve one press manned by four to eight workers. The primary issue was production standards, although questions of health and safety arose as well. A majority of the workers in department 19 were engaged in these actions at one time or another. The new hires provided the impulses, and some of the slightly older guys provided the organizational thought and practical initiative. "In a way," Kord notes, "they worked as a team." None of these actions lasted longer than a day, usually ending within a couple of hours or less. Some of the "strikes," in fact, lasted only a matter of minutes. Kord describes a prototypical wildcat as follows:

After lunch you might notice a certain set of presses not operating. Word would reach the chief steward or me. The spokesman usually turned out to be the steward (Johnny Zyznomyrsky). He didn't always initiate these things, but when he saw there was going to be a wildcat he would join and take the initiative, riding in on a wave of feeling.

You go in to negotiate. The guys are standing by the presses. "What's the grievance?" you ask. "Production is too high," answers a spokesman. "These guys feel they should be getting more money at this machine over there because of the nature of the work." "Now wait a minute," went a typical reply. "We just signed a contract. You can't go ahead and rediscuss the wages we just agreed to."

Or, if Kord (or Vasdekis, Shannon, or Pinkowicz) thought that the demands were justified, he would bring the matter up with the bargaining committee, and they would renegotiate that part of the contract. Such changes as occurred were always negotiated. "Sometimes the committee, whether they thought it was just or not, would try to get a compromise just to have peace in the family. Sometimes the company would go along to have some peace."

There were real inequities, Kord points out, and often the wildcats got results over standards. For example, the necessity of close coordination among the six to eight men working a multiple press created a great deal of tension. Each time the press was raised, the piece of work had to be passed along to the next man and placed in position. But not all of these lifting, twisting, and placing operations were the same, and one worker could have had a more difficult task than another.

There was a good deal of *solidarity* among the guys on the presses. They lived together in the neighborhood, they drank together, and they had been or still were members of neighborhood gangs. They faced the chief steward or the president as a solid group. For his part, Kord (when the task fell to him) had to convince their spokesman and mollify the group. He might tell them that the committee would take up their complaint with the management. At that point the spokesman would turn to the guys and say something like, "The committee is going to go up and see what they can do." Thus mollified, the workers would return to their presses. Activity of this sort was not carried out in hostility to the union leadership; it was an effort to get some special consideration, sometimes deserved, sometimes not.

As Kord saw it, the wildcats did not always fit in with the best interests of the union. In union meetings the wildcat element would discuss standards of production, not rate of pay (which they preferred to handle through the wildcat if they could). Standards, not wage adjustments, others could sympathize with. But the union leaders thought that this method of handling grievances was

rather harmful to the organization and its broader goals; for one thing it exploited and magnified the problems of a small group of people when we could be handling their problems and everybody else's problems through the organized channels. . . . We didn't like the idea of handling one department at a time; and then, having handled one thing under pressure here, you are going to get pressure in other spots, lose control of the whole situation. A broader vision was defined. The leadership understood that you had to have everybody together to be effective.

The question thus raised is, What was the *historical character* of these wildcats? Formal political, programmatic, or organizational efforts, even of the most rudimentary kind, were completely lacking. There was no planning—not even in bars—although some informal complaining in a local bar might precede the wildcat. There were no meetings, no caucuses, no efforts to involve the rest of the shop. As a first approximation, then, the workers could be described as historically inarticulate. Though volatile and militant, they existed on a low level of historico-political activity. One person or a few people started the wildcat. The preexisting gang structures, the feelings of solidarity, and the volatility and readiness for action of the second-generation Poles supplied the existing undercurrent, always present, which made possible these almost spontaneous actions. The wildcats never spilled over into another department. Without anything like a program, with demands that were always localized, without the broader issues on which alone it would have been possible to appeal to other workers in the shop, their influence remained slight.

In addition, the wildcatters never ran candidates for office, although in department 19 leaders would emerge. However, the choice of leaders was not the result of an ideological or political process; they were simply the more popular, aggressive, and articulate workers. Eddie Dobrovolsky, one of the earlier hires whose seniority in department 17 went back to 1932 or 1933, was the most important of these leaders. He "had a following, a small group" in the middle of the shop. About a dozen workers in departments 17 and 19 looked to him for leadership, although "it wasn't a definite group all the time." By 1938 he had become a steward on the afternoon shift in department 17. Because the main leadership was on the day shift, he "had a clear field on afternoons." There was some overlapping with the barroom brawlers and certainly with the gang structures, and a strong loyalty to the group and to the leader.

It is precisely in this capacity that Johnny Zyznomyrsky was unique among the secondary leaders. Hamtramck-born, he boasted of never having been outside the municipality. In a sense he was the embodiment of the spirit of the young second-generation neighborhood Poles. He was the preeminent leader in the press departments and had stuck his neck out earliest. He had good rapport with his people and had effective control of his department. It is instructive, therefore, to examine his relationship to the wildcats, for they were expressions of a historical tendency—of a definite capacity to act in a specific (and presumably radical) way. And thus the organizational and ideological manifestations of this tendency must be studied. In so doing, the historical immaturity, the unformed social and political character of the wildcatters, becomes clear. For Zyznomyrsky was ambivalent, torn between his past milieu and associations in the press departments, and his present (and future-oriented) activity. If his past was Hamtramck, the neighborhoods, bars, and gangs, his future was the union: Kord, Vasdekis, and the others. Sometimes he led a wildcat; but often he was easily convinced by Kord or Shannon to return to work, and sometimes he even felt sheepish about the whole affair. "When he led the wildcats, they were more effective, since he was the steward and could wield a wider authority in the department. On the other hand, he became apprehensive when they seemed to get out of hand. He never whole-heartedly supported the tendency.... In a way, Zyznomyrsky was caught in the middle, but he also enjoyed this kind of thing."

The strategy of the leadership in approaching the wildcats is indicative of their weakness as a tendency. Vasdekis, Pinkowicz, and Kord were not merely of the same opinion in how to deal with wildcats, they shared a similarity of mood. Shannon, on the other hand, though never disagreeing with the other three on the question of what position to take, was less serious, more tolerant. Thus Shannon was frequently assigned the task of talking down the wildcatters. "They listened to him, he would give them some kind of moral dispensation. Where I would get serious, Shannon would smile and joke."

Furthermore, the second-generation press operators themselves were divided over the wildcats. Not only were the gang kids a "significant factor" in the wildcats; even among the earlier hires it seemed to Kord that it was the younger workers who were more involved. Kord's guess is that it was the second-generation with families who "by and large would work toward restraint, but when the wildcat erupted they would go along." Overall, about 50 percent of the second-generation workers in department 19 "didn't really go along" with the wildcats, although there was "group pressure on them," and once an action was initiated "you didn't break solidarity." Nevertheless, these workers were "reluctant" before and felt "sheepish" after the wildcats. Such attitudes were "another reason why we could defuse things eventually, without too much trouble." If one weakness of the wildcat tendency lay in its inability to produce a full-blown leader who directly and unambivalently expressed it, another was found in the limitation of its appeal to the youngest workers in the plant—workers who had yet to fully leave behind their adolescent associations and social perspective.

# CHAPTER SIX

# Consolidation

IN ITS EFFORT to expand and consolidate its position in the plant the union had to extend and strengthen its influence among two very different social groups. Not only was it necessary to bring the remaining holdouts into the union, but the political character of the center of anti-union strength, the toolroom, had to be changed. Thus, soon after the last holdouts were forced into the union following the dues strike of the spring of 1938, the leadership initiated a strategy of sending solid union people into the toolroom as apprentices. The fear and indecisiveness of the first-generation workers also posed a serious problem. How reliable would they be in the event of a sharp confrontation? Such a confrontation materialized in November of 1939, when the union initiated a slowdown over its demand for a paid vacation. The successful outcome of the dues strike, the colonization of the toolroom, and the slowdown not only securely established Local 229, but the union acquired almost undisputed power in the shop and to a remarkable degree usurped the authority of the management to control the process of production.

## The Dues Strike

The subtle and not-so-subtle pressures that the union militants put on the holdouts soon after the contract were generally successful. By the spring of 1938 only about twenty-five workers were still outside the formal structure of the union. Yet to the leadership the situation was not as rosy as it might have appeared. "We felt insecure as long as we didn't have them all in," Kord remembers. "We were a very suspicious bunch then." The leadership thus determined to force the remaining holdouts into the union. Their tactic was simple: after a certain day, they announced, the union would prevent nonmembers from working by stationing a part of the "flying squadron" at the gates to check dues receipts. "We created the impression that this was it." As a result all but three of the holdouts joined the union. For the leadership—indeed, for the broad ranks of the union members—this was not enough. The union prepared for a confrontation.

As Kord saw it, there was no doubt about the seriousness of the threat that inhered in the situation. "It was psychologically important [to get the three holdouts into the union]. If we didn't get them in . . . eventually [the company] would water down [the union]. They would get other people into a frame of mind of not belonging, maybe five, ten, or twenty, but the company knows how to use these things too." The holdouts would have continued to function as stool pigeons, and the company would have looked for additional ways to use them. There was always the problem of the holdouts' being able to prey on the periphery of the union, on the members who were not part of the solid core of cadre or militants, by simply talking to them, saying something like, "You sucker, you pay money and we're not, and we're getting the same thing that you're getting. The union didn't get that for you, the company gave it to you." Most of the leadership, understanding the situation in precisely this way, considered it imperative to get the three holdouts into the union and were willing to shut down the plant.

The rank and file were solidly behind this effort. The whole plant knew that on the appointed day there would be a large number of hefty guys checking dues receipts, and nobody was going to get in without one. This met with general approval; the man who was paying dues resented those who were not though nevertheless receiving the benefits of the organization.

It is important to note that the three holdouts were not acting on their own. The company was encouraging them in their resistance, and the issue was thus sharply drawn. On the final day, when the union strong men appeared at the company gate checking dues receipts, the management panicked and shut down the plant. This was definitely a blunder, for as Kord sees it this made the company appear to be the aggressor. The union, its position enhanced, turned the lockout into a strike in which there was complete solidarity. Yet the outcome of this strike was not a foregone conclusion to Kord. As he sees it, the strike was a crucible in which the character of the union would be tested for the first time, in which the leadership would find out whether or to what extent it could depend on the postcontract members, the first-generation workers, the Appalachians, and the inspectors and toolmen. "We had never had to depend on the whole union in a struggle like this. Here, by closing down the shop to force three holdouts into the union, we were going to find out if we really had a union: it was the moment of truth. After that we could go on to other things."

The strike was short, lasting only a few days. The union told the management people that since they were the ones who had closed the plant down, there was only one way of reopening it. The management, surprised by the effective response of the union and having been unprepared to wage a long battle over this issue, put the pressure on the three holdouts to join the union. A further surprise must have had its impact on Bergson and Perkins: the appearance at the plant of numerous UAW militants from other locals. The early spring was a period in which precisely such "dues strikes" were breaking out in a number of plants;[1] the Local 229 strike, Kord remembers, was one of the first in the area, and the picket lines were swelled by a large number of volunteers from other locals.

One of the most important consequences of the dues strike was the disappearance of the reluctance which still characterized the first-generation workers' attitudes toward the union. At this point they became more dependable union members, although "we weren't sure of them yet, even though they were members." Yet, though a degree of fear had been removed by this successful struggle and the first-generation workers integrated more solidly into the organization, their attitudes toward authority were not significantly transformed. The company had precipitated the dues strike and encouraged solidarity by its aggressive action. But how would the first-generation workers respond in the event of a direct contest of authority in the plant between the union and the management? Such a test would come in November of 1939.

## Colonization of the Toolroom

Around the time of the dues strike or perhaps a few months afterwards, the union initiated another program of consolidation: the colonization of the weak departments, especially the toolroom. This policy, however, emerged only gradually out of a number of *ad hoc* decisions. "Some of the active people, early militants, who had no position [in the union], started looking around for opportunities. The idea developed, perhaps some of these people could be used in areas where the union was weak. . . . We knew that if we got some good guys in there we would change the character of the department." The union's strategy involved putting in a bid for one of its loyal members each time an opening appeared in inspection, maintenance, or the toolroom. In the period before the war this was made easier by the fact that the toolroom was being expanded, new jobs put on, and openings created.

But this policy could cause problems if it appeared as a mass movement; guys in the toolroom would fear for their jobs. The union thus had to move slowly. The policy developed within "the top layer and the people close to them," including most but not all of the secondary leaders. "If enough people knew about this—and there were enough—they'd look for situations . . . and see where there was likely to be an opening." The plans did not "filter down all the way, just far enough so that we would be able to find relatively good young guys to go in there. . . . We didn't want to make it obvious that we were colonizing, because that would have created a political problem." Those who were aware of what was going on included the decision-making leadership group, workers who might be in a position to transfer (and whom the leadership had already picked out as likely candidates), and union members who could help create the desired situation: the stewards and the most reliable militants in a department. Through these connections the leadership kept its eyes open for some likely candidate. This was a "one-way street: we would to to the candidate, not vice versa (although perhaps Wilson was an exception to this. This was likely to be a thing that would come up in a small group meeting, a committee meeting or a top leadership meeting. Somebody would say, 'Now here's a good guy, what about him?' (The guy wasn't present at the meeting.) Basically, this was the way it happened." Because the policy was applied very slowly, because no one used the word "colonization," because the policy, in fact, was not actually conceptualized and verbalized as such, few people knew what was going on.

The leadership started choosing men for these positions, all the time waiting for an opening to occur. "We wouldn't let [the company] hire new people," Kord recalls. "We would say to the company, 'Let's look around the shop first.'" The union always had a couple of candidates waiting for each opening. The company, for its own reasons (which were ambiguous), went along with the idea. There was no use of union pressure; the leadership dealt mainly with the foremen and the shift superintendant in these discussions. If they recommended the assignment, it would most likely go through. The leadership wanted to get decent union men into these positions, yet they could not lay the union open to charges of nepotism. The workers had to have capabilities, but the union made a conscious decision not to promote union leadership. Under the circumstances it involved walking a fine line. The workers who were promoted were rank and filers who had stuck their necks out early. All were moderately active and belonged to some group of organized workers.

Why did the company so easily accede to this proposal? The first colonizer in the toolroom was Elmer Wilson. Driving his electric truck around the plant, delivering messages and actively aiding in the early organization of the local, he was undoubtedly a thorn in the side of the management, and Kord suggests that the company may therefore have had an ulterior motive in removing Wilson from this position and dropping him down in the middle of a thoroughly anti-union department. When Kord was transferred to inspection in 1940 (in order to get on the afternoon shift so he could continue school—there was no increase in pay), part of his motivation was to colonize inspection; but the company, Kord suggests, may have wanted to isolate him in the same way that Wilson might have been isolated in the toolroom.

That things did not work out as the company seeemed to have planned was shown in the subsequent history of the toolroom. At least four others went into the toolroom during these early years: Michael

Letkiewicz, a second-generation Pole who came from department 17, characterized by Kord as "very good, reliable, and quite active, but no hothead"; Joe Wasielewski; and maybe one or two others who were "quiet, not very active, but faithful." These additions were enough to change the character of the toolroom, enough so that "we were never threatened with any major uprisings there. (Incidentally, we got a lot of information on the toolroom from them. We were able to size up every individual in there after a while.)" Furthermore, "we managed—I haven't figured it out—to get Wilson elected steward early in the game, in spite of the fact that he was an import, he was younger, and he was a strong union man. What gave us the opportunity was the fact that we nailed the first president." Wilson ran against Luebke for steward and beat him. Kord surmises that Luebke may have made enemies in the department. Even though Wilson was known as a strong union man, therefore, he had a definite advantage over Luebke. But Wilson ran for steward before several of the other colonizers entered the department. A number of factors, not all apparent, must have contributed to this *coup*. First of all, the non-union workers never put up one of their own: their opposition was anarchic, individualistic, without energy, and consequently historically inarticulate. Secondly, the union was established and had already demonstrated that it meant business when dealing with recalcitrant workers who themselves had been pressured by the union toughs to join and who had seen the power of the dues strike. Thus they may have considered it wise not to oppose the union in any too easily identifiable form. Finally, as the job of the steward includes handling grievances the interests of the toolmakers were best served by having a steward who was aggressive and capable of doing a good job. Yet Kord notes that Wilson might not have lasted except that several other colonizers later joined him, and Wilson therefore had the most cohesive grouping, despite its size (six or seven members of the informal "union caucus"). And he must have been a diplomat, Kord concludes, to have been able to stay on for as long as he did (throughout the war).

The toolroom accounted for the larger number of colonizers, the total of which for the entire shop was between eight and ten. All of the Slavic colonizers were second-generation workers; no new hires were among them. What sets these men off from the others was their sobriety of temperament. Wilson, in fact, not only did not drink much but was a religious Catholic—as we have seen, an uncommon trait among the workers in the shop, most of whom were only nominal Catholics. Steve Porkonicki, a second-generation Pole who went into the maintenance department, was a solid union man, although he had not been an early activist and was never overly active; he was "sober, calm, conscientious, nothing flashy, a family man, and he never drank too much."

Many of these colonizers had significant occupational qualifications. Letkiewicz and Wasielewski were setup men, and Wilson had been a setup man once before. "Setup was a stepping stone to a very large extent." Porkonicki became an electrician's helper after starting in department 17. Wilson, Letkiewicz, and Wasielewski stand out in Kord's memory because they were the "best leaders" in the toolroom. However, Kord thinks that their sobriety and family centeredness were characteristic of the other colonizers as well.

Among these colonizers two, Wilson and Letkiewicz, joined the Socialist party. Wilson, as we shall see, was one of the earliest people to do so. Compared with the others, he had a better grasp of politics (presently, he writes a column for a local UAW paper). Letkiewicz had not been very active as a secondary leader before the contract, nor was he very aggressive. "He . . . worked in a minor key and was very loyal. . . . He wasn't much of a speaker and was close to Johnny Zyznomyrsky and Frank Jaskiewicz in the quality of his socialism."

The social characteristics of these men suggest that there is a sociological as well as political dimension to the process of colonization. Colonization was also *pari passu* a form of upward mobility for a certain element of the moderately active, more sober and conscientious second-generation Slavs, and it provided the political framework within which some of the more individuated and "Americanized" second-generation workers broke into the skilled industrial trades hitherto monopolized by workers of WASP, Irish, and northern European background. Although the union's responsibility for the personal advancement of these second-generation workers inevitably intensified their loyalty to the organization, this factor cannot be isolated and subsumed under a concept of "opportunism." Instead, one of the main themes

running through the history of Local 229 is the complex interconnectedness of a number of tendencies. It was precisely these radical,
more individuated workers who took the lead in organizing the union.
Agressively seizing opportunities and bent on self-improvement, they
nevertheless pursued their aims within an egalitarian and broadly social-
democratic framework. That they saw no contradiction in this is an
indication not of their lack of integrity or insight, but rather of the
weakness of much of radical theory itself. The problem of interpretation that this poses is dealt with in the broader context of chapter 8.

## The Slowdown

In October 1939 Local 229 entered into negotiations with the Detroit
Parts Company over the terms of a new contract. The union shop,
standard seniority and grievance clauses, and a minimum of seventy-five
cents an hour for production workers as well as sixty-five cents for
sweepers were agreed upon without the eruption of sharp conflict.[2] But
when it came to vacations with pay Perkins and Bergson balked.
Perhaps a third of the UAW contracts by this time included vacation
clauses, and Local 229 raised the demand for equal treatment.[3] In
discussions with Bergson (Perkins did not participate) the company
"not only refused to give us a vacation, but offered philosophical
reasons to the contrary. Mr. Perkins, we were told, simply doesn't
believe in vacations for workers." It was clear that the union was
getting nowhere through negotiations. Other tactics were thus deemed
necessary.

Calling a strike, however, seemed unwise. The question of unemployment compensation was up in the air.

We knew that in a strike there would be no unemployment compensation. What happens in the case of a lockout? This was not clear . . . so
we decided to have a slowdown, and if we were going to close the plant,
it was going to be the company that did it. [Furthermore] in a
slowdown we would have our people still in the plant; we'd have them
where we could work with them more closely. On a picket line,
everything is decided immediately . . . and you don't know how they're
going to react. We [had] never had a general strike. . . . What if some

people decided they didn't want to go on strike? A slowdown was so novel an idea that it seemed to be more acceptable at this point. This is how it began.

The decision and its implementation were carried out by the top leadership. There was no discussion with any other workers "because you don't discuss this kind of detail . . . because this alerts the company . . . [and enables them] to counteract before you do it. You've got to take them by surprise."

After Bergson announced to the negotiators that Perkins did not believe in vacations for workers, Kord and the others went downstairs and discussed the matter with the committee. The discussion lasted about an hour, after which "we passed the word to cut by five percent."

Each committeeman was in contact with some of the stewards, and the stewards "obviously were waiting for the committee—they always waited for the committee to come down, eager for some news. They probably had a feeling that something was going to be done, but they didn't know exactly what. When we decided to cut by 5 percent word quickly got around; the stewards acted responsibly. There was no discussion. The stewards carried out orders, but word had passed around. When the workers found out that Perkins didn't believe in vacations for workers," their anger aided in the maintenance of discipline.

"Five percent was easy, a game, it wasn't even very noticeable. The company was taking production at the end of the day. We didn't tell them there was a slowdown, didn't tell them anything. We just kept cutting deeper. We knew they'd have to notice at some point. When a day's production was turned in they'd have to notice there was lower production. Over the next several days the union cut deeper and deeper. The second day the cutback amounted to 10 percent; then 20 percent; then 25 percent"; then, in one or two more steps, 50 percent. When the union got down to one of these latter figures, the boss gave his instructions: get the count every hour. "When we found that out we decided that every hour we'd have a count. Every hour on the hour everybody would go to his machine and run one piece. Then they'd go back to playing cards or what have you." This was the situation in the middle of the second week of the slowdown.

Finally, "there was an urgent need in the shipping room to get out fourteen bundles of goods to Chrysler. Now one guy could have loaded fourteen bundles in ten minutes flat. Since it turned out that there weren't enough people in the shipping room to get the job done in a reasonable time at the rate of one bundle per hour, the company went out and got men from other departments and had them form a line. With enough men it was obvious that they would be able to get the truck loaded." So for every worker carrying a bundle, the union attached to him another worker whose task it was to take the bundle off the truck and return it to the stack. Why go through with this charade? "If the company was asking production every hour, and there was no production in one hour, the company could call this a strike. This way, we were in a position to say that there was some production." (Kord is "not sure they were reading [Perkins and Bergson] right, but why would they be taking production every hour? So we decided, if they were taking production every hour, we would have some production every hour.")

The truck never got loaded. Bergson "was walking back and forth, looking very worried." Kord was also finding the struggle exhausting, although he had hardly the same worries as Bergson. "Look, Mr. Bergson," Kord finally said to him. "You don't want to lock us out, and we're not going to strike. Why don't we agree that . . . the plant will stop operating, and the union and the company will get together and discuss this issue of vacations, and it will be neither a strike nor a lockout." Bergson heaved a big sigh and said, "Yes, let's do that." The leadership got the word out: "Everybody goes home. This is not a strike, it's not a lockout. We'll be talking."

Richard Frankensteen, director of UAW Region 1, sat in on the meetings for the UAW. For the first time, Kord notes, the union met with the president of the company in his paneled office.

[Perkins] was one of those gruff speaking guys, [and] he was mad at us. He wasn't going to talk with us, he was going to talk with Dick Frankensteen, who was representing the International then. Perkins turns to him and says, "Dick (as if he had known him all of his life), you know (Perkins shows Frankensteen a stack of papers on his desk) I've got enough work here for these guys for fifteen years—at the rate they're going! I've heard of slowdowns before, and I've heard of slowdowns of 10 percent. Do these guys slow down 10 percent? Nah, never! Do they slow down 20 percent? Nah, nothing like that! They don't slow down 50 percent. They get down to one piece an hour! I'm going to take this paper [the production report] and put it up on the wall. Nobody ever did that before!"

Frankensteen starts laughing, his belly starts shaking. At one point I decided this wasn't going to be a two-man conversation, so I start putting my two cents in, and Frankensteen says, "Look, what they're asking for is not being unreasonable. We just got a vacation in other plants, and they're asking for a paid vacation. That's not unreasonable." After Dick talked for a while Perkins said, "All right, I'll give them a vacation—three days, but they've already had it this year." He said this slowdown was a vacation. At this point I said, "Mr. Perkins, I never had as tough a job to do as this slowdown. Don't think it was a vacation, to me it was a very hard job. We didn't have a vacation." Perkins finally agreed to a three-day vacation, and it would not be considered that we had had it already.

This was the hardest work anybody ever did—getting through this thing. It sounds easy, one piece per hour, but to sustain this kind of thing when you don't know what move is going to be made next is not easy, it's nerve-wracking. The first day was fun, at least for the leadership. The second day it's not so funny, the third day it becomes—well, now you're playing for keeps and you can't afford to make mistakes. Some of the guys go through the whole thing, just following orders, and it's fun. But for the guys who have the responsibility it becomes a real hard job for them. It's exhausting. You had to get word, yourself or somebody else, see that orders were carried out, see that nobody broke discipline. And we had the first generation who were generally scared. They went along. The second generation was inclined to see more fun in it from the beginning. The first generation went along, but they wouldn't see it as that funny, because they were afraid of consequences. But they were good union people, so they went along. Somebody was making decisions, giving orders, and they went along. They were religiously following it. They weren't making fun, but the younger guys would razz the foreman a little bit, or sit down and play cards.

By now these first-generation guys see that the union is solidified, they have seen the results, they know that the company is afraid of the union, not vice versa. The first act of defiance of the first generation is going along with us in the slowdown. It was the first time the first generation had to take a stand where there were consequences. By now the older guys, who had never lost their fear, realized that the union was here to stay. They lost any hesitation they might have had. Afterwards, whenever we had a strike, these old guys were the old faithful, they were on the picket line. They were on the picket line religiously.

As far as the young guys are concerned, it sort of went to their heads, it was heady drink.

## Aftermath

With the successful conclusion of the slowdown, an epoch in the life of the local came to a close. It had achieved stability and permanence based on a power that, within the framework of the plant itself, was almost unconditional. Following the slowdown, a thrust toward workers' control that had been slowly developing markedly accelerated. By the middle of the war years the company had completely lost control of the production process. The union set up a group incentive system which made it impossible for an individual to compete with his fellow workers. Moreover, unlike many other incentive systems (which were really speedups), the 229 plan was run by the workers themselves, and it led to a situation in which ten hours' pay was received in return for a *maximum* of six-and-a-half hours of work. Often these hours were considerably reduced. In order to accomplish this, however, it was not sufficient to exercise the negative power of the strike or the slowdown. Increased productivity was required. Workers' control, increased productivity, and a relatively nonrepressive system of in-plant relationships constituted the three social and political pillars on which this system rested. *The union took over all managerial functions on the shop floor.* This fact is of far greater significance than either the unanimous resolutions favoring a labor party passed by the local or the consistent opposition to the wartime no-strike pledge, both of which were political statements reflecting, as we have seen, the preeminent role of the leadership in shaping ideological positions. In contrast, the control of the shop was a far deeper and more thorough manifestation of praxis.

Without exception, upheavals even as limited (in terms of political and social practice) as that of the 1930s come about as a consequence of and also result in severe dislocations in the social structure: in the structures of authority and repression and in the structure of culture and everyday life. Like a miracle, a germ of humanity, of species being, nourished in the warmth of the freedom suddenly attained, strikes root in the lives of ordinary people, gives them hope and encourages their aspirations, fires their imaginations and broadens their conception of self until it embraces mankind as a vivid, sensual reality to be lived in the empirical world. Yet the fundamental contradiction inherent in such periods of upheaval and reform must be faced: objectively, certain possibilities were ruled out, others were inevitable. The historical character of a movement can be quite distinct from and even opposed to its more radical episodes. It is this contradiction that now concerns us.

# CHAPTER SEVEN

# Culture and Structure

IN THE TWO-YEAR PERIOD following the signing of the first contract, the structure of leadership within the union became increasingly formalized. It achieved a remarkable stability, based on the successful integration of a heterogeneous group of 450 workers into a common political, social, and cultural life. The leadership considered the primary task to be the achievement of unity, a unity that had to be forged despite the immense differences of culture and outlook in the plant. Essentially, a viable coalition needed to be formed. At the beginning of this period, in the fall of 1937, such a process had only begun. The formal leadership structure was established, although it remained restricted to the leading cadre of the precontract period. By the end of the two-year period, however, the enlarged institutional structure of the union provided an organizational outlet for the more ambitious workers. Finally, there was the emergence of a group of Socialists around Kord, a circumstance that affords us an opportunity to examine the nature and significance of working-class allegiance to radical parties within the framework of the local union.

### Leadership and Bureaucracy

From the outset the leading cadre who had initiated the early struggle emerged as the dominant element in the shop. The officers, the committeemen, and the stewards were drawn from this group. In the following several years not only was there a relative stability of union officers, but in plant elections the leadership often "gave the nod" to the candidate it favored, usually with the desired results. This was a delicate situation. The nod was not always taken, and sometimes the leadership decided not to give it when someone else was likely to be elected anyway. Giving the nod was not considered necessary in every case; it was done "when it was thought that it would make a difference and when it wouldn't create sharp issues." The leadership's policy was not to intervene more forcefully than this, but in every department before elections people who were close to the leaders consulted with them. Often this was the way the nod was given; or a guy who wanted the job might have looked for support from the leadership. As it turned out, most elections took place by acclamation. There was a lot of discussion before the election, and the outcome was no surprise. In most cases, in fact, only one candidate ran.

Even in the midst of apparent turnover, an essential stability existed. In front-welding, for example, no one remained steward for long: the position rotated, by gentlemen's agreement, among King Kong, Bill Lewis, Cooper, and Pinkowicz. Nick Buglaj remained steward of department 16 for a number of years. Johnny Zyznomyrsky remained steward in department 19, Lew Thompson in shipping, and Leo Ptasz in torch-welding. Frank Jaskiewicz left department 17 and moved to the transportation department, where, Kord thinks, he took Wilson's place as steward. Wilson (the first steward of transportation), as part of the union's policy of colonizing the toolroom, moved to the latter department where he replaced Luebke as steward. In department 18 Zero was the first steward, where he remained for a few years. The stewards that followed him were all second generation. In the inspection department either John Yadlowsky or Charles Watson became the first steward. Neither of them was associated with Al Schein; certainly Yadlowsky, and probably Watson, joined the union before Schein brought in his group. In the years that followed, however, there was a relatively high turnover of stewards in the inspection department, with Al Schein returning to a position of influence during the war, when he was elected steward.

The bargaining committee was the most important functional organ insofar as direct relations with the management were concerned. It was to this committee that the stewards brought their major grievances. The committee was thus entrusted with the responsibility of negotiating grievances between contracts as well as bargaining the terms of the new contracts. Elected by the general membership for a yearly term, the composition of the committee was closely controlled by Kord, Vasdekis, and Pinkowicz. Their policy included developing flexibility and a system of rotating the members of the committee while always maintaining a majority that was both experienced and close to the leadership. Thus, Shannon stayed on the committee, Pinkowicz was on most of the time, and Vasdekis some of the time, while Wilson, Jaskiewicz, Adams, Steve Porkonicki, and Harry Kozik, all solid union members and loyal to the leadership, alternated the "loose" positions. In spite of occasional contention for positions on the committee, its basic character remained what the leadership desired it to be.

A further concern of the leadership was frankly political. The committee was always balanced geographically, with a representative from every part of the shop. "We wanted to have ears, influence all over the shop," recalls Kord. "No part of the shop should be able to say, 'We were not represented.' " Sometimes, however, the question of representation came up, with some department asserting that it deserved to have a representative on the committee. As Kord saw it, "the committee was a place where moderate change and turnover could be afforded. We didn't want the committee to appear ingrown, but we always kept a core of experienced people."

Delegates to the UAW convention were chosen from a fairly small group of five or six. "When we got to the meeting we had our candidates selected already, and everybody else from among our people would decline. If anybody wanted to run he didn't have a chance because the news was out." At first, the two delegates were selected from among Vasdekis, Shannon, Kord, and Pinkowicz. Later Jaskiewicz and Kozik were added to this select circle. The primary leadership made the decision, the secondary leadership accepted it, and there were no questions from the others. The meeting was a "rubber stamp affair."

The four major offices were the most stable of all: throughout the war Kord remained president, Shannon vice-president, Pinkowicz recording secretary, and Vasdekis financial secretary.

To what extent can we call this state of affairs *bureaucratic*? The only alternative to the isolation of the union cadres and the disintegration of organization was the institutionalization of the impulses and tendencies that had gained the initial victory. To some extent, this institutionalization was the residue of the period of formative activity. Yet *bureaucracy* seems overly charged with pejorative overtones. The militant members who occupied the leading positions in the union were widely respected and trusted, and for their part these leaders were themselves closely tied to the workers in the plant. Even Kord, who was considered "odd" by most of the workers, quickly became a part of what was in fact a close-knit community coexisting within the institutional structure of the union. And if the division of labor within the union gave the appearance of bureaucracy, the leadership was nevertheless intent of widening the base of active decision-making, culminating by the end of the war in an executive board of fifty workers. What must above all be recognized is that at the outset the union suffered from a shortage of experienced and capable leaders. Kord, Shannon, Pinkowicz, and Vasdekis had brought to the situation personalities that were capable of assuming responsibility immediately, but for many of the others, the union itself proved to be precisely the educational and character-forming experience that would result in the creation of a much broader base of experienced and capable cadre.

Thus the problem with the use of the term bureaucracy is that it conjures up an image of something else, of a formation distinct from and perhaps even opposed to the workers in the shop. Yet in the case of Local 229 the bureaucracy was almost precisely the sum total of the most forceful, intelligent, committed, and farseeing union men in the shop. It was thus not a structure external to the drive for organization, but was rather the formalization and institutionalization of that very drive itself. It was predicated on the assumption that although a minority of the workers had brought the union into being, a substantial majority could be integrated into its social structure. Toward this end, the ability of the union to guarantee job security through seniority and grievance procedures was perhaps *the* critical factor. And the successful erosion of the authority of the management, described earlier, implied the establishment of the authority of the union. Such considerations are critical in seeking to understand the impact of the union on the development of the Appalachians, the first-generation Poles and Ukrainians, the toolmakers, and the inspectors. If the militants of the press departments were part of the originating forces that brought the union into being, the first generation and the Appalachians were instrumental in having made possible its survival and establishment. But, unlike the militants, the latter workers remained relatively passive though loyal union members, and they played their part only through the mediation of the leadership; insofar as the allegiance of these workers brought about united action, the leadership occupied a strong bargaining position. As a result of the passivity of these two groups as well as the political immaturity of the wildcatters and the indifference or hostility of the majority of non-Slavs, the active political life of the union was confined to a small circle of second-generation cadre. Under these objective circumstances, the leadership enjoyed, if not autonomy, then at least a wide latitude. If the ultimate boundaries within which it could function were in the last analysis fixed by broad historical tendencies and by the aspirations and perspectives of the rank and file, in the short run it was not always clear that this was so.

### Ethics, Morality, and Attitudes Toward Authority

The striking differences in attitudes toward authority exhibited by the first- and second-generation Slavs help make intelligible the development of the local. In relation to the foremen and the manager the first-generation worker exhibited feelings of deep fear and submissiveness, in spite of an equally strong hatred and resentment. When a foreman approached a first-generation worker the latter, if not working, hurriedly and furiously began; if working, he sped up his pace. If smoking, he immediately crushed out his cigarette; if talking, he broke off in mid-sentence.

On the other hand, the second-generation worker ignored or talked back to the foremen and went to the can when he wanted to. If not working when a foreman passed by, he returned to his machine or to his task but in a more leisurely manner. He finished cigarettes and sentences, and he was the first to break the three-minute (!) lunch rule. This sharp contrast in behavior seems to be unaccountable in terms of circumstances alone. Even after the contract, when much of the objective source of fear had been removed, the attitudes of the first-generation worker remained unchanged, while those of the second-generation worker were dramatically transformed.

What is so striking in this regard is that when conflict arose within the union and there occurred an implicit if weak challenge to the leadership, this constellation of attitudes persisted. The first-generation workers rarely spoke up at union meetings, and after the dues strike in the spring of 1938, they were the most loyal and dependable supporters of the leadership. They could always be relied upon to man the picket lines, although they were almost never involved in the outside work of the flying squadron. In the course of a dispute within a local meeting they generally remained silent, perhaps one or two saying a few words of support for the leadership. In voting, they were almost unanimous in their support of established authority. The choice of words is deliberate, but by no means do I intend to suggest that a simple transference of attitudes occurred. Rather, attitudes and patterns of relating to authority, in regard to both the management and the union leadership, seem to have deep roots in a common peasant-communal experience. A remark of Kord's is immensely suggestive. The first-generation workers "trusted me . . . I was kind of their father-confessor. They'd come to me with their problems. For one thing, I was a little bit of two worlds, so I understood them better and they understood me better. They came to me with their personal problems" (family and financial problems, as well as those relating to the outside or to dealing with social agencies). On the other hand, they hated the management and had tremendous respect for the leadership, especially Kord. The union itself meant a great deal to these Slavic immigrants, and their loyalty was sincere; it grew out of a basic identification with the aims of the union.

It was primarily the younger of the second-generation workers of department 19 who were the source of much of the factionalism—a factionalism that brought with it a number of attitudes that we have already seen in relation to the foremen: the militants were outspoken, self-assertive, and fearless. They were "more willing to take chances, especially the local people from the neighborhood gangs. They didn't figure out the effect of their demands on the total picture. They thought that every demand was legitimate, [that] anything was possible." They were more actively involved in union meetings. And they could not only be relied upon to man the picket line but also relished participating in the action of the flying squadron—to a great extent they *were* the flying squadron of Local 229.

Yet both the first-generation workers and the wildcat element of the second-generation workers failed to produce any leadership. Although the language problem prevented the first-generation from running for steward, for example, they almost without exception depended on others to undertake all responsibility.[1] The wildcatters had their leaders in Johnny Zyznomyrsky and to a lesser extent Eddie Dubrovolsky, and never aspired to any leadership positions themselves.

The Appalachian migrants seemed to combine some of the characteristics of both the first- and second-generation workers. They had nothing to do with the militant wildcatters, yet they were also more outspoken and more outgoing than the first-generation workers. They were not cowed by the foremen, yet they did not participate in the early struggle. Like the first-generation workers, they loyally supported the leadership.

Basic differences in morality, ethics, and culture lay behind these varied responses to the questions of authority and discipline. Such issues must also be seen as centering on the basic problem, yet to be worked out, of what the union would be. And it was in union meetings, when the Appalachian workers, the first-generation workers, the wildcatters, and the militant cadre interacted, that four distinct cultures or subcultures, four separate perspectives and styles of being "union," emerged.

These differences became most apparent during discussions of the "illegitimate" demands raised by the militant wildcatters involving a violation of the contract in the interests of a particular group. ("Legitimate" demands are defined by Kord as centering on the terms of a new contract: the amount of the wage increase, the nature of seniority, and the framework of time-study.) The discussion might grow out of a wildcat or more often out of an attempt to alter the seniority system between contracts. In considering a proposal the militant wildcatters had a frankly pragmatic appraoch: "will it work?" was their only concern, referring to a wildcat, a violation of some provision between contracts, or anything else. There was a kind of nihilism that Kord noted, together with a rudimentary code of "solidarity and fighting the company." The Appalachian migrants, on the other hand, responded quite differently. Whenever they thought something was wrong they expressed themselves vociferously, characteristically saying, "It ain't right!" (for example, in regard to an attempt to alter the terms of the contract by violating them). A strong sense of individual morality was expressed. Furthermore, they had no sense of society as such but couched all their thinkings about social and political issues in individualistic and specific nonpolitical terms.

The first-generation Slavs rarely responded vocally to the nihilistic behavior of the militant wildcatters, yet as we have seen they consistently supported the leadership. When they conceived of a question of right or wrong, it was an ethical rather than a moral problem: they thought in terms of social right or wrong, speaking sometimes about the rich and poor, about the big employers and the workers, sometimes about socialism. Even in relation to the militant cadre (Cooper, Lewis, King Kong, etc.) these workers seemed to Kord to have a higher political consciousness. Unlike the Appalachians, therefore, the first-generation workers had a concept of society and ideas about how society should be run. Among them was a group of twenty or thirty, perhaps more, of old country Socialists (whose sympathies were with Pilsudski rather than Luxemburg). They were able to talk about socialism, the rights of the workers, and sometimes even Communism (some expressed pro-Communist ideas); they read the literature and once in a while went to a mass meeting. This difference in political and social consciousness was not great, but it was perceptible. They could discuss the smaller parties, they had heard of E. V. Debs, many of them had experienced the 1905 Revolution, and they knew about the Russian Revolution of 1917. Yet in many important respects they did not differ from the other first-generation workers. Their fear of the foremen was the same as that of the non-Socialist immigrants, and there was no difference between them in their response to authority. With the exception of Buglaj, they never provided leadership, confining their activities to that of faithful followers. Like the rest of the first-generation workers, they loyally manned the picket lines but never went to another strike. "These people didn't like wildcats . . . and would support us on those questions. But . . . if we had an organized wildcat or some kind of action that was illegal . . . that was supported by the top leadership, they would go along with us."

It is now possible to recapitulate in summary form some of the main cultural currents in the plant. The leadership cadre was rational, calculating, aggressive, self-disciplined, and possessed of an impulse for self-improvement. The political form that these characteristics took could be described as a kind of social democracy, linked uncertainly at first to the New Deal as its left wing. These workers had the highest development of social and political consciousness, in contrast to both the Appalachians and the young militant wildcatters. The latter group possessed little if any political consciousness. Instead, pragmatic and adventurous, they idealized both combat and solidarity. On the other hand, they seemed nihilistic, narrow in their perspective, and, if self-sacrificing as individuals, they sometimes appeared in union conflicts to be self-centered as a group. Yet their primary identification was the union, which to them, however, seemed to be something of a bigger and better gang. For all the chaos they brought to the local situation, they were among the shock troops of the union, the militant fighters who went out to other picket lines and to demonstrations.

The Appalachians were individualistic and moralistic; the parallel with their fundamentalist sectarian cultures is to the point. They were deeply loyal to the union after it was established, yet their allegiance was expressed within the framework of a powerful individualistic morality and as such must be clearly distinguished from the very different kind of loyalty of the first-generation workers. For the latter the *community* was the focal point of primary identification. The Appalachians had had to be convinced one at a time to join the union; once persuaded that it was *right*, their loyalty was unbounded. The first-generation workers, on the other hand, saw in the union an extension and politicization of the community. Thus, the communal-ethical culture of the first-generation workers, the individual-moral culture of the Appalachians, the nihilistic fraternity of the gang kids, and the rational-cosmopolitan praxis of the union cadre were, as a first approximation, the four major currents of pro-union activity. As for the other workers—the toolmakers and the inspectors—some became good union men (although these tended to be inspectors rather than toolmakers), while perhaps a greater number of skilled Protestant workers who participated in the union could be characterized as individualistic and opportunistic and others—those whose membership was involuntary—could be described as individualistic and anomic.

These cultural currents could take on an implicit—that is, unconscious—political form. Both the inspection department and department 19 functioned as definite social entities, although neither was self-consciously organized as such, and each was sharply different from the other. I have already described the forms of group and neighborhood solidarity of the young press operators in department 19 and the role of Johnny Zyznomyrsky as group leader and spokesman. Unlike any other department, 19's workers were drawn from the immediate neighborhood of the plant. If the relationship to the union of the second-generation welders and helpers was on a more rational (that is, ideological) and individual basis, that of the young press operators in department 19 took the form of a group affiliation or federation, in which at first (and less consciously) what was a mere mood or tendency took on definite form. Johnny Zyznomyrsky not only became the leader of the subculture that department 19 contained, but it was precisely through him that the relationship to the union was mediated. It seems therefore proper to refer to this informal cluster based on a common subculture as having *affiliated as a group* with the union (this is how Kord sees it), the latter being represented by the leadership cadre. On the other hand, the inspectors, particularly the non-Slavs, were drawn from all over Detroit, and few lived in Hamtramck itself. We have already noted that after a while Al Schein was able to reassert his ascendancy, becoming a steward during the war, and that he had some influence, both in his own department and in nearby cutoff, which he used in an effort "to keep trouble from happening" (to prevent strikes). It appears that here Schein became the spokesman for an informal tendency which, precisely because it expressed a kind of individualist culture threatened by the Slavic union, found it necessary to coalesce around him. In this case, as in the last, there was a mediated relationship to the union, but on an entirely different social foundation.

The political structure that arose out of the cultural makeup of the work force appears paradoxical. The wildcat element, which included a number of earlier hires as well as new hires in the press departments, was opposed at union meetings by a coalition of the militant cadre, the first-generation workers, and the Appalachians. Two characteristics of this situation are immediately noticeable: the second-generation workers were divided (although not deeply), and the militant cadre was supported by the most conservative, or at least nonmilitant, groups of pro-union workers. The Schein group, outside this informal system of political association, played an independent conservative role which, however, sharply differed from that of the first-generation workers, who were the most deeply loyal group in the plant. Though fearful of confrontations, they stood fast as a solid bloc once the confrontation exploded in the fall of 1939. The Schein group included people whose "loyalty" was to a large degree based on pragmatic considerations of the realities of power, and it was always a weak spot in times of crisis, although it abided by the rules and remained within the legal framework of the union.

## Socialists, Catholics, and Syndicalists

The Socialist party grew only among Kord's circle. The whole group around Vasdekis remained isolated from Kord's direct influence, while Pinkowicz and the Catholic group were hostile to socialism, Pinkowicz himself never "quite accepting me all the way." The cultural and political divergence of the Vasdekis and Kord groups, hinted at earlier, became more pronounced. The differences that existed were "complementary," Kord notes, and there was never any conflict between them. From a practical standpoint, therefore, these diversities were of little significance. To the historian, however, they provide a valuable opportunity to observe closely the fine structure of leadership as a social process.

Pinkowicz was the focal point around which a small Catholic group coalesced, although the ties were weaker than those of the Kord and Vasdekis groups. Pinkowicz "was a man of some importance. I'm sure that all the strong Catholics in the shop had a lot of respect for him." Steve Porkonicki and Zero were close to him. A number of other secondary leaders were Catholic and non-Socialist. "I'm sure that there was a group of those people, but they were scattered over the shop." Pinkowicz was thus the informal spokesman for a Catholic element in the shop.

If Pinkowicz had been undermined, the union would have lost the respect and support of some of the Catholics. [He was] in the Vasdekis group, even though he was different from them. He had to be in that group . . . to be a leader. He had to find a *modus vivendi,* even though he was as different in relation to them as I was in relation to others. Pinkowicz stood somewhat to the side. He had about their education, was a milder man, and was not physically as strong. He was a very, very strong Catholic. (Vasdekis, if anything, was anticlerical.) Pinkowicz was the least willing to use muscle in the whole department. If Vasdekis and Pinkowicz had a vital point of disagreement in the department, the guys would go along with Vasdekis. [There never was any such disagreement, as Kord recalls.] There never seemed to be a complete leveling between him and me. He had a reserve about him.

This "group" of Catholics, composed largely of younger, second-generation Poles, had almost no influence among the first-generation workers. After the war they formed the nucleus of an Association of Catholic Trade Unionists (ACTU) in the local, held their meetings in the basement of a church, and unsuccessfully sought to remove Kord and the Socialists from the leadership of the local. (In fact, the ACTU generally had little success among the first generation, gaining much of its Slavic support from among the more Americanized workers of Slavic descent.)

The group around Vasdekis—King Kong, Cooper, Bill Lewis, Alice the Goon, and Sawdust—"looked at him as a very decisive man who knew his mind, a man who was a maverick, but a guy who was very much like them, just somewhat more capable and decisive, that's all. Actually, that was a very close-knit group, a very ingrown group." In terms of their approach both to politics and to trade-union questions they could best be characterized as pure and simple shop-floor militants. If they went along with the UAW's policies of support for the Democratic party nationally and for pro–New Deal labor slates locally, their lack of involvement with politics and their emphasis on direct struggles on the shop floor distinguished them from both the Socialist and the Catholic groups. Although they undoubtedly never used the term, the people around Vasdekis were a tough band of syndicalists.

Under what circumstances might Kord have been able to recruit some of the Vasdekis group to the Socialist party? Even if Vasdekis had not been there, Kord would not have been able to recruit anyone. "But if I [had] cracked Vasdekis, he would have brought over a few people. He had greater control of those people than I ever had. If I had been at loggerheads with Vasdekis, I would have been at loggerheads with them. But if he had come into the SP, he could have brought some of them, but not all of them." Kord, speculating further about this possibility, noted "that if that had taken place, they would have remained tied to Vasdekis, they would not have acquired the broader outlook" that Kord was able to provide his people. Group ties were very strong. Kord never tried to do anything about weaning these people away from Vasdekis, and he never invited anyone from the front-welding group to a Socialist party meeting. Only through his general propaganda activities in the shop did Kord have any contact as a Socialist with the Vasdekis group. Kord had once asked Vasdekis to join the party, and he had refused. After that, Kord made no further attempt as a Socialist to contact the front-welding group.

In contrast, the Socialist party group "aspired to acquire more ideas and more ways of building a union and more ways of building a labor movement in a world where labor would matter more. They looked out of the shop more, they would see a broader picture than the people in the welders." And the people around Kord had "more drive," becoming increasingly active in the work of the union. In addition, there was a great deal of occupational mobility among the Socialist party group. Kord went into the inspection department (although basically because he had to go on afternoons in order to fit in his class schedule), Kiertanis left the presses and went into welding, Jaskiewicz moved from the presses to transportation, and Wilson moved to the toolroom. All of these were advances within the occupational structure of the plant.

Kord had come from a Socialist, anticlerical family in Poland, and, although at the time of the organizing drive he had had no contact with Socialists in the United States, he certainly had the background and disposition that might lead to involvement. Around the late summer or early fall of 1937, Kord discovered a leaflet for a Socialist party meeting and decided to attend with the intention of joining. There were some union activists present at the meeting, but workers were in the minority. Thus began Kord's involvement with the Socialist party in Detroit.

By the end of 1938 Kord had recruited Shannon, Wilson, and probably Zyznomyrsky to the Socialist party. He believes they joined probably on the basis of personal loyalty, rather than a deep understanding of socialism. In the following few years Buglaj, Jaskiewicz, Adams, and a few others joined. It must be noted that all those who came into the party were drawn from the leadership cadre, and the question is posed, What precisely was it about Kord that attracted these workers to the Socialist party? If ideological understanding was lacking, as Kord observes, is it not possible to conceive of their relationship to Kord as in some sense political? Those attributes of Kord that stood out most clearly in the local situation included rationality, self-discipline, education, political consciousness, and organizational ability. Insofar as Kord identified himself with the Socialist party, to the workers of the shop it was not the party as such, but rather that part of it which they saw reflected in Kord, which attracted them. Nor was this misleading: in his personality and behavior Kord *was* an adequate embodiment of much of what radicalism represented. Thus, joining the Socialist party was not merely an ideological commitment, but rather an identification with a certain mode of being in the world, a striving to transform one's personal and social practice in accordance with the ideals that Kord directly, and the Socialist party indirectly, represented.

These recruits to the party subscribed to and helped Kord distribute Socialist papers and occasionally signed up new subscribers. "The light we were putting on the Socialist party through our activities is that the party was really another side of the labor movement, that there was a very close connection between the two—which wasn't exactly so." The party in Detroit was divided into two branches. Branch 2 was the labor branch, and its meetings were attended by the 229 Socialist party members. The discussions at the meetings generally covered such topics as the UAW, John L. Lewis and the CIO, issues within the unions, and activities that Socialists were having in different locals. There were no theoretical or ideological discussions—these took place in Branch 1, whose members were bourgeois elements; teachers, lawyers, and businessmen. The education meetings were likewise the province of the intellectuals of the party; the 229 workers never attended them. "From what they saw of the SP it was a pro-union thing. They knew of the middle-class elements and would meet them at picnics. . . . When there were good speakers like Norman Thomas they would listen." There was friction between Branches 1 and 2. "Branch 1 wanted a pure approach to the labor movement . . . it was more 'left.' The people in Branch 2 didn't want to seem ingrown, wanted to spread out, and couldn't come out too radical. They wanted to be close to the people."[2]

Although the Local 229 members of the Socialist party developed politically to some extent, they never became "first-class Socialists." All of the most active secondary leaders under Kord's influence joined the party. They included Shannon from torch-welding, Zyznomyrsky and Kiertanis from department 19, Jaskiewicz from department 17, Wilson from transportation (and later the toolroom), Adams and Kozik from inspection, Buglaj from swaging, and LeSante from shipping (and later the toolroom).

The Kord group exerted a subtle influence on a few people who in temperament would seem to have been closer to the Vasdekis group. A number of wildcatters looked to Shannon rather than to Kord; others, who tended to go along with the wildcats, were close to both men. Stanley Blaskiewicz, who became steward during the war, was among the latter. Eddie Dobrovolsky, although part of no group, got along well with Shannon. Consequently, it was usually Shannon, at the request of Kord, who talked him out of a wildcat. Shannon thus was the "syndicalist" face of the leadership. His good standing with the wildcatters, despite his being an integral part of the Kord Socialist party group and his success in dealing with them, is another indication of the historical character of this wildcat tendency. Furthermore, much of the contact that the Kord group had with Vasdekis was through Shannon. Kord notes that the two seemed to share a similarity of temperament. Shannon, Zyznomyrsky, Dobrovolsky, and Vasdekis and his group lacked the ambition that characterized most of those in the Socialist party group, and with the exception of Dobrovolsky, who got onto the committee during the war, they persisted in both their precontract roles and their occupational statuses. Thus, with the exception primarily of Vasdekis (and to a lesser degree, Shannon), these syndicalists played a fairly subsidiary roles in their capacities as leaders. If they tended at times to view things differently from Kord, they nevertheless spontaneously accepted his judgment and leadership. And as the objective situation changed following the contract and consolidation, these men were eclipsed by new leaders.

Both Walter Adams and Frenchy LeSante emerged into important leadership positions only after the early struggles and the establishment of the union. Adams, we recall, was unable to play an early role because of his isolation in inspection, though he was among the first inspectors to join the union. LeSante, one of the first in his department to join the union, was limited in his activities by the isolation of the shipping department before the contract. Later he became steward (in 1939) and went into the toolroom (Kord is unsure whether he was a colonizer). He became quite active and "was a very important guy on the safety committee." Both of these men lacked the toughness and thirst for battle that characterized many of the early leaders. Temperamentally, they were more at home in the institutional setting that developed after the contract. Yet it would be incorrect to characterize them as opportunists. Their attachment to the cause of the union was genuine and spontaneous, they had taken risks before the outcome was known, and their role in the later stages of the union's development must be seen against the backdrop of the changing objective character of the situation. Inevitably, the success of the early struggle compelled a change of circumstances; these men were suited to carrying out the work of the union under the altered circumstances, while the original ideals and motivations of the early struggle remained intact.

It was quite otherwise with Charles Watson and Harry Kozik. Watson had not stuck "his neck out early in the game" and "was not at all in contact with the leaders during the struggle. . . . I think he got into the union at a time when he decided that this was going to be most likely a success, and he decided to make the most of it." He became steward on afternoons in the inspection department soon after the contract, but he did not really move up until the war, at which time he got on the bargaining committee, later becoming the union's full-time time-study man, a position of great importance. He was a bit of a politician and grew quite popular. He was talented, had a lot on the ball, and was ambitious. He was an opportunist to some extent, yet he "made a real contribution to the union."

Harry Kozik did not become actively involved until after the slow-down of 1939. He was one of the early joiners in the press departments (but not among the earliest), though he did not really make his mark until he went to inspection. He emerged into leadership activity early during the war, when he got on the committee and joined the Socialist party. Kozik "was open for bids" and "went where his best interests lay." A "careerist," he was more "self-seeking" and later became a foreman.

Because of the Kord group's dominance in the shop it seems inevitable that these new men should be attracted to it. Opportunists such as Kozik and Watson, of course, always seek out the centers of power, while LeSante and Adams undoubtedly found the rationalism and stability of the Kord group congenial.

Whether or to what extent this subjective difference between Adams and LeSante on one hand, and Kozik and Watson on the other, was reflected in their roles in the union is problematic. The basic purposes of the union had already been established, and its political character had already been formed. Problems of a relatively technical and routine nature dominated the administrative and executive practice of the union, and new men rose to occupy the leadership positions which the early syndicalist leaders had neither the desire nor the ability to assume. Thus, to the new men both the structure and the functions of the union were accepted as given; and though perhaps a sharp historical crisis might have divided the Adamses and LeSantes from the Watsons and Koziks, under the existing circumstances it was difficult to objectively distinguish them.

The new men had a drive and ambition that distinguished them not only from the syndicalists, but also from the militant cadre of the Kord Socialist party group. All of them dramatically improved their occupational status. Kozik got into inspection and later became a foreman,

LeSante went into the toolroom, Watson became the union's time-study man in the plant, and Adams, an inspector, was elected president of the local after the war, later becoming a banker and a city official in Hamtramck.

Thus, between the spring and summer of 1937 and the postslowdown period, there unfolded far-reaching changes in the constellation of forces and in the character of the union itself. Most indicative of this evolution is the degree to which the new men eclipsed the old. Only the four primary leaders, plus Jaskiewicz and Wilson, wielded more power than these new men, although in fact Adams moved ahead of Jaskiewicz and Wilson, and Watson's position as time-study man was perhaps more important than all but the top offices in the union. It was only on the lower rungs of secondary leadership that the original muscle and spirit of the dramatic first months of the union's life remained. There were still to be found Lewis, King Kong, Cooper, Zyznomyrsky, and maybe one or two others. Kord, Vasdekis, Shannon, Pinkowicz, Jaskiewicz, and Wilson, of course, embodied in their experience, personalities, and relationships to other workers that genuine spontaneity of feeling, fraternal affection, loyalty, and commitment that continued for many years to characterize the life of the local. But the contradiction remains: in the bureaucratization and specialization of functions and in the rise of the new men, the union had indeed changed.

# CHAPTER EIGHT

# Conclusion: The Union and the Outside World

THE OBJECT of this study—the investigation of the nature of class, the emergence of leadership, and the formation of institutions—seemed best served by adhering to the strategy of a minute investigation of a single local. To assess the character of the industrial labor movement, it was essential to examine the internal structure of relationships within the working class as a key to the inner logic of its development, and the local union was a proper region of investigation. It was on the shop floor that the basic infrastructure of social and political relationships emerged upon which the institutional and political structure of the International depended. Within this region questions of culture, religion, and personality, as well as leadership, politics, and structure, can acquire a concreteness lacking in both the institutional studies of Fine, Bernstein, and Purcell, for example, and the populist-syndicalist studies of such authors as Brecher and Aronowitz.[1]

Because of this theoretical rather than narrative purpose, an emphasis was placed on such processes as bureaucratization and the rise of the new men, whereas in the subjective experience of the workers themselves such perceptions were nonexistent. The fraternal life of the local was just beginning to emerge, a rich system of friendships and associations was developing, increasing numbers of workers were becoming drawn into the work of the union, and an executive board of fifty members was being created in an effort to provide greater opportunities for active involvement. It was an admirable local, militant and democratic, whose spirit of goodwill and solidarity had grown strong in the course of the struggle.

Yet the truth of a historical process may not be found in the experience of its subjects. From a theoretical viewpoint the genesis of a historical tendency, its spontaneous and imperceptible beginnings, is of primary interest. If the mass movement is conceived of as an organism, the study of its genesis qua structure implies an attempt to conceptualize its genetic code. Thus, the purposeful theoretical intent of thick description has the effect of the culmulative piling up of subtle changes in emphasis, and can have a sharp impact on the ultimate impression, precisely because the objective is *theoretical*, rather than impressionistic (or naïvely empirical). Behind this purposeful intent of description is the knowledge that the full implications of a movement may not be apparent until its immanent dialectic has concretized itself in further praxis. If the history of Local 229 was part of a broader process extended in time as well as in space, its significance can emerge only as these contextural relations become clear.

Yet except for Fine's painstaking institutional history, much of the writing on the heroic years of the UAW has been enthusiastic and uncritical; and none of it has posed the real problematic contained in its history: the formulation of the appropriate concept of its inner development. To do this requires the realization that the structure of the UAW, as it unfolded in the forties and fifties, could only be understood by an analysis of its roots in the structures set in motion in the formative years. These structures, moreover, could only be grasped within the region of the local union viewed from the standpoint of the interior of the factory itself. Thus, it is the organic connection between the present and the past that poses the problematic of the UAW; and if the structure of the UAW in the postwar period can only be understood by referring back to the thirties, conversely, the real character of the movement of the thirties could no longer be sought in its appearance, but rather in the dialectic of its development, as this is posited in the course of its history.

There are, of course, objective limitations to this study. The problem of boundaries laid out by the region and the historical space dealt with is significant. Determining which substructures are appropriate in the larger analysis is also essential. Although the social and political life of the local was fairly insular, it was enveloped by a historical context wherein powerful forces were at work. In many ways the local became a microcosm within which the basic impulses of the New Deal were elaborated. The intense attachment of immigrants and their children to the New Deal was one of the foundations on which the CIO rested. Even the Trotskyists acknowledged this: "Our policy"—Trotsky is speaking to Farrell Dobbs and James Cannon—"is too much for pro-Rooseveltian trade-unionists. . . . The danger—a terrible danger—is adaptation to the pro-Rooseveltian trade-unionists." "The 'progressive' rank and file are a kind of semi-fabrication. They have class struggle tendencies but they vote for Roosevelt."[2] To this "Jeb" adds: "On the question of adaptation to Roosevelt's program by our trade-union comrades. Is it true? If so, it was necessary for our trade union work. The trade unionists are for Roosevelt. If we want to make any headway we have to adapt—by not unfolding our full program—in order to get a foothold for the next stage."[3] During the 1938 Michigan gubernatorial campaign, in which the UAW was supporting liberal Democrat Frank Murphy, Kord spoke up in support of the Socialist candidates, but to no avail. Even in his own local he was unable to make a dent in the overwhelming support of the Slavic workers for the New Deal and FDR. Because the new immigrant masses formed the CIO leadership's most reliable base, the left-wing tendencies of many of the leaders were sharply confined by this objective fact of political life.

This commitment of the new immigrant masses had its structural correlates in the internal organization of the UAW. Failure to conceptualize these concrete structures of working-class practice opens the way to ideological projection—a familiar result in much of radical labor historiography. But to the degree that these concrete structures are articulated, the problem of conceptualizing the historical character of the labor movement—and of the working class—becomes in theory soluble. While it is correct to note the distinction between the working class as a social formation and the labor movement as a particular sectional organization around specific political and institutional objectives, the task of analyzing the historical character of the working class in a particular epoch is dependent on an analysis of the specific concrete structures of working-class practice. Where these structures are of a limited trade-union character, one must, in the absence of any other structures of historical articulation, comprehend the negative as well as the positive significance of this fact: the absence of a broader, more political working-class practice—in the form of the structures appropriate to this practice—must be studied in the space opened up by this negativity: in the concrete structures of parochialism, anomie, nativism, and passivity.

The objective in what follows is to use this account of Local 229 as a point of departure, seeking to conceptualize the historical character of the working class itself in the automobile industry through the drawing of inferences on the basis of the present study supplemented by other materials. The first step, however, is to situate the local within its institutional context in relation to other structures in the UAW. We have already seen from the point of view of the factory's (and the local's) interior that despite the fervent commitment of the rank and file of Local 229 to the New Deal and the broad consensus on this point within virtually the entire UAW, the local to a great extent was isolated from the political life of the UAW. This was true even of the secondary leaders. As we have seen, the choice of convention delegates involved almost no discussion by the rank and file. When Vasdekis was one of the convention delegates (in the early forties), he tended to vote with the Left (which included George F. Addes, R. J. Thomas, and Richard Frankensteen), yet the assumption that this action reflected anything about the character of the workers thus represented by Vasdekis would be entirely unjustified—although Vasdekis did represent the views of his immediate constituents, the group in front-welding. Even Kord, who as a member of both the Socialist party and the Unity Caucus might be expected to have been more deeply involved in the political struggles that rocked the International from late 1937 through 1939,[4] responded more directly to the practical needs of the local than to the political needs of his caucus. The lack of obvious materials in the relation of the local to the UAW should not mislead us into thinking that the relationship itself was unimportant. In the absence of obvious political ties, there remained nevertheless the structure of that relationship of apparent political indifference. We thus turn our attention to the body immediately superordinate to the local union: the regional office.

## Region 1

Region 1 of the UAW, covering Hamtramck and the east side of Detroit, was the administrative body immediately superior to Local 229.[5] Until the spring of 1938 the region, under the leadership of Richard Frankensteen, Morris Field, and R. J. Thomas, was associated with the Progressive Caucus of Homer Martin. Local 229's immediate contact with the UAW (especially during the first year) was with Field, and Field was loyal to Frankensteen. Johnny Ringwald, Local 229's service representative from the Hamtramck District Office, was a loyal Martin supporter (in contrast to Frankensteen, whose attachment had a more pragmatic character), who continued as such even after Frankensteen and Field went over to the Unity Caucus.

The most important fact about Region 1 may well be its emergence out of the company unions (the Works Council) inspired by the National Recovery Administration and set up by the management throughout the Chrysler Corporation toward the end of 1933. By the spring of 1935 a majority of the delegates elected to the council, fed up with their lack of power under the rules established by the company, organized the Automotive Industrial Workers Association (AIWA),[6] although it was not until January of 1937 that all of the AIWA representatives resigned from the Works Council.[7] An examination of the list of candidates supported by the AIWA for the positions of delegates to the Works Council, as well as the list of candidates for office at the First Annual Convention of Delegates of the AIWA reveals a preponderance of old immigrant and native American names.[8] Among the leadership of this group were Morris Field and Richard Frankensteen. The close association of the AIWA with Father Coughlin, and a nativistic, anti-Communist speech given by Frankensteen at a mass meeting in Belle Isle Park in 1935, give a strong indication of the influence of Coughlin's depression-born brand of populism, nativism, and anti-Communism among certain groups of workers in Detroit.[9] Coughlin's support was heaviest among old immigrant Catholics and Lutherans, and was considerable among working-class Protestants.[10] Since it was not until the end of 1936 that the union had any influence among the mass of Polish workers in the Dodge plant (and this was slight before the sit-down of March 1937), the political weight of these early members was decisive in the formation of the leadership structure. The predominance of native-born and old immigrant names among the stewards, committeemen, and executive officers of the Dodge local even after the great uprising of 1937 is indicative of the character and structure of the organization in its early years.[11]

Although the trim shop, the most strongly organized department in the Dodge plant,[12] was to become the center of left-wing strength in the local, the most decisive section of the AIWA milieu tended to be socially and culturally conservative, including in its ranks a large number who expressed an aversion to the kind of centralized, radical, national organization that the United Automobile Workers represented. Both Richard Harris and Richard Frankensteen have noted that there was a "sharp internal fight"[13] over the proposed amalgamation with the UAW, which was accomplished in May of 1936, 35 percent of the members of the AIWA opposing the merger.[14] The results of the Dodge local's elections of May 1937 for officers and plant committeemen show the Frankensteen forces (soon to be linked with Homer Martin in the Progressive Caucus) defeating the emerging left wing (and soon to be pro–Unity Caucus) by about two to one. Out of twenty-seven thousand workers in the plant, only ten thousand voted.[15]

After the March 1938 elections, in which a Progressive slate backed by Frankensteen went down to defeat before the Unity slate (a consequence in part of the broader involvement of the Polish masses in the political life of the union), Frankensteen moved over to the Unity Caucus, a switch that was no doubt encouraged by the election results.[16] Although the social and political character of the Dodge local underwent a transformation, the old AIWA leadership cadre continued in control of the regional office, while Johnny Ringwald, with whom Local 229 had its major contacts, remained with the Martin-dominated Progressive Caucus. Because of the nativist, antiforeign, and anticosmopolitan character of the Martin faction, virtually no active immigrant or immigrant-stock workers were involved, with the exception of a few who identified strongly with the native, English-speaking Catholic cultures. The Unity Caucus, on the other hand, made its most energetic appeals to the foreign-born, and thus it would seem that as far as the

Slavic workers of Local 229 were concerned, the issue would have been clearly drawn.

Yet the location of Local 229 in Hamtramck, the home of the plant's Slavic workers, the overwhelmingly New Deal character of the municipality—in government as well as in popular sentiment—and the political revolution in the Dodge local itself seem to have had little effect on the behavior of the local in relation to Region 1 and the factional dispute. Although profoundly committed to the New Deal and the CIO, the rank and file and even the leadership of Local 229 were fairly apolitical when it came to the UAW and internal politics. Until the final split between the Progressive and Unity forces, and the separate conventions of the spring of 1939, a host of nitty-gritty practical considerations were uppermost in the minds of the local leadership, while ideological considerations counted for little. "We weren't very factional," Kord notes, "until the fight became very sharp. We knew there was a big fight, we knew it was dangerous, but how everybody was lined up we didn't really know. We weren't all that political, internally." Even to Kord "the whole situation was really unclear. The details were unclear, certainly." Kord was not as "politically aware in 1938 and 1939 as [he] would later become." Thus, despite Frankensteen's move to the Unity Caucus and the collapse of the Martin forces in the Chrysler region, Johnny Ringwald continued to enjoy the support of the leadership of Local 229.

In many ways the leadership of Local 229 considered Ringwald's technical service of vital importance. Ringwald was present at the first contract negotiations, and in the months to follow "he helped settle some of the problems we had. He was involved with the backwash of some of the slowdowns and wildcats." Ringwald "functioned as an experienced consultant. He would come and help the committee with some of these problems. Remember, people were not trained and were new at this thing. The service reps do more than just help negotiate a contract. They help with everyday problems that arise, and they are called on more to the extent that the local people can't handle them." "At the beginning we weren't sure of ourselves, we needed the help of the rep, and in the first couple of years our main contact with the UAW was with someone like Ringwald." In addition to these problem-solving contacts, the local met with Ringwald at its monthly membership meetings during its first two years. This continued through 1938. Then "we started doing more of our own work, became gradually independent, [and] acquired skills." Ordinarily the representative had contact only with the top leadership of the local, especially Kord and Vasdekis.

This personal contact with Ringwald overshadowed all ideological considerations. "If Frankensteen had gone with Martin," Kord conjectures, "despite my wanting to stay with Unity there might have been a division in the local, with others wanting to go with Field and Frankensteen. They were more interested in servicing the local than the high politics of it. If they were getting good service and if they weren't put on the spot by the reps they would have been interested in not rocking the boat because they had problems in the local." And Kord adds, "I'm not sure that if I had been satisfied with the service that I would have gone along with the lines of factionalism. I don't know." When the division in the UAW occurred in March of 1939, Ringwald had already lost the trust of the local leadership, in part because he began holding secret meetings with the management, in part because he carried an instrument of nonverbal persuasion to union meetings, and the local sent its delegates to the CIO-Unity convention in Cleveland on March 27, 1939.

Two letters, written by John Vasdekis to a high-ranking official in the UAW, give eloquent testimony on the character of this situation. The first letter was written in early March, when the Homer Martin faction was holding its rump convention in Detroit. Stating the results of the local elections, the letter went on to note that "factionalism was a stranger as far as the good will and solidarity of Local 229 were concerned"; it then announced a charitable donation made by the local to a sick brother and reported other bits of local news, mentioning the fact that "Johnny Ringwald of the International acted as chairman and swore in the elected officers."[17] Later that month the letter appeared in the *United Automobile Worker*.[18] The reference to Ringwald had been deleted.

The second letter, undated, but obviously written between April 14 and April 18, 1938, is far more revealing, and I quote it in full.[19]

Mr.____

As you no doubt know our local [h]as been working under the direction of the Hamtramck District Office which is under the care of John Ringwald.

Until recently we have disagreed with Mr. Ringwald on factionalism, but when it came to local affairs we always found Ringwald ready to go to the limit with us even so far as keeping factionalism out of the local.

We would like to know if there is anything we could do in so far as keeping Ringwald in this office.

In the past we found that most organizers didn't care to have much to do with small locals such as we have in our district, and therefore we would like to keep a good organizer here while we have him.

If this letter is considered factional or political, disregard it, as we have had to[o] much factionalism and politics already.

The reason this letter is being sent to you instead of anyone else is because you['re] the only one I've ever written to and in my judgement [you will read this letter in the spirit] in which it was written.

Hoping I'm not doing the wrong thing in sending this letter I remain

Fraternally Yours,
John Vasdekis, Secy Tres
Local 229

## The Auto Workers: Cadre and Radicals

If the above account of the broader political practice and organizational relationships between rank and file and the leadership cadre on a regional and national scale is valid for other locals (and so far I have come across no evidence to the contrary[20]), far-reaching implications follow. With the historical practice of the mass of workers confined to the local and characterized by a political and organizational passivity (even the wildcat element had no political articulation and was confined to a single department), the more historically articulate and powerful expressions of working-class struggle were situated in the leadership formations, and even these formations were highly differentiated. Their character and their specific relationship to the rank and file are therefore a matter of great theoretical importance. When the formation of these bureaucratic structures can be considered an essential moment in the unfolding of the movement itself (and not imposed from without on a reluctant working class), the question of class and that of bureaucracy are necessarily linked.

By far the most significant practice of the whole movement, insofar as practice enjoyed some degree of national organization and poltical effectiveness, was to be found in this bureaucracy. Composed of the most active and aggressive part of the working class, the bureaucracy, in the last analysis, can perhaps be considered the chief product of working-class struggle itself. With a minority of workers actively promoting the cause of unionism, and with a majority remaining either passive supporters or opponents of the union, the most significant objective factor conducing to the formation of bureaucracy was found both in the narrowness of the base of active involvement and in the breadth of the more passive mass that was brought under the jurisdiction of the union. In addition, the transference of patriarchal attitudes toward authority on the part of a large number of workers provided the historical and psychological nutrients out of which bureaucracy could grow. No doubt there was a good deal of working-class activity that had no bureaucratic consequences. In Local 229, however, the most highly articulated form of such activity that had any historical weight was the wildcat tendency, yet we have already seen how weak this tendency was. Restricted to a milieu of young second-generation press operators, the wildcats had considerably abated by the time of the slowdown of November 1939, while at the same time the syndicalist elements around Vasdekis were increasingly eclipsed by the rise of the new men. In short, the study of bureaucracy is bound up with the study of the most active cadre of the movement itself.

One is struck by the spontaneous inevitability of this process of bureaucratization. Within the plant the local's center of gravity was found in the early cadre within which the semiskilled workers were prominent—with exceptions such as Kord further emphasizing the specific social differences between the cadre and the mass—and in the bureaucracy which to a great extent grew out of this early cadre. In the organization of other locals as well the centers of gravity were similarly circumscribed. In Flint it was the trimmers in the body shop who took the initiative and provided the main base of the pre-1937 organizing efforts.[21] In Briggs it was the metal finishers,[22] in Studebaker the frame builders,[23] in Dodge the trimmers and cushion builders,[24] in Hudson and Packard the metal finishers.[25] These men were the most highly skilled and highly paid production workers in the industry. Moreover, they were finding that what had once been something of a skill and even a trade was falling under the double onslaught of speedup and rationalization.[26] Wages of these workers were $1.00 to $1.10 per hour, compared with an hourly rate of sixty-five to seventy-five cents for assembly and other unskilled work. In addition, Anderson and Rightly, speaking of their own experiences in Studebaker and Briggs, note that the early cadre of the semiskilled workers was on the whole far more temperate than the other workers in the shops.[27] This may have been generally true.

Among the more active pre-1937 unionists native American and old immigrant workers were preponderant, while Poles, blacks, and Appalachians were relatively underrepresented. Yet the distinctions to be made are not ethnic, but sociological. Although the active rank and file of the AIWA and later the UAW in the Dodge local conformed to the above description (based on an examination of delegates lists, candidates lists, and interviews), there were a number of Polish militants who occupied leading positions. Joe Adams's grandfather had come to the United States before the Civil War, Adams's father had been the editor of a Polish-language journal, and Adams himself was a trimmer. Walter Rogowski worked in an unskilled department although he himself was a mechanic. Joe Ptaszynski was a key organizer in an unskilled assembly department, an area of relative union weakness. Ptaszynski, however, had been a tool-and-die maker driven into unskilled work by the depression. All three shared an urban, cosmopolitan background, possessed skills, and were therefore quite distinct from the mass of agrarian immigrants. There is reason to suspect that workers of Polish background such as Adams, Rogowski, and Ptaszynski (as well as Kord) were the ones who threw themselves into the union struggle early in the game and who played a more active role, in contrast to the mass of agrarian immigrants, who joined after the big strikes and who, as we have seen in Local 229, were loyal but passive union members.

The sociological and historical counterparts of Edmund Kord himself seem to have been scattered throughout the automobile industry. Of those leading individuals whose oral history interviews I read at the Archives, eight of the ten came from petty-bourgeois backgrounds. Paul Russo, one of the three early leaders in the Nash plant in Kenosha, Wisconsin, originally got his job in order to save money to go to college.[28] Leon Pody was a ruined small-business man.[29] Bud Simons had had a garage of his own during the depression, but had to go back to work in the plants.[30] Harry Ross's father had wanted him to go to college, but Ross refused and got a job instead.[31] John K. McDaniel, the son of a mining engineer, had a college education.[32] Richard T. Frankensteen's father was part of the Dodge management, and Frankensteen himself was a college graduate.[33] Richard Harris's father was a cashier in a bank, and Harris himself had been in the insurance business before adversity forced him into the plant.[34] Tracy Doll had been a salesman who was driven into the plants when his company folded.[35] More generally, the importance of such declassed petty-bourgeois elements has been noted by Edgar Lock.[36]

Likewise, the growth of the Socialist party in Local 229 was in its basic features similar to developments elsewhere. While the external policies and ideologies of the several left-wing movements diverged sharply, there were, on the shop floor and within the UAW, more similarities than differences. Within the unions the radical parties were seen by their new shop-floor recruits as made up of the most determined and capable exponents of trade unionism and the most democratic and militant forces within the New Deal.[37] As Kord and Marquart point out, there was a tension in the Socialist party between the ideological middle-class "left" and the pragmatic trade-union "right" (if these terms mean anything). The Communist leadership had problems, too.

We have the problem in several cities, as Dayton, for example, of some splendid trade union members who have joined our party but do not see the party except as a necessary force to help them organize the trade union. . . . Very many workers have joined the party because of their support for our immediate program, our leadership in the struggle against fascism for peace. They may not yet understand the broad implications of our People's Front policy. They may not yet understand the ultimate aims of our Party, as the Party of socialism.[38]

Trotsky, discussing the state of the Socialist Workers' party work in the CIO, noted that "many comrades are more interested in trade-union work than in party work," and he goes on to warn that "it is an historic law that the trade-union functionaries form the right wing of the party." They "deal with the class, the backward elements . . . the pressure of the backward elements is always reflected through the trade-union comrades. It is a healthy process, but it can also break them from their historic class interests—they can become opportunists."[39] A rare unanimity among such bitter enemies!

True, some of the older cadre in the Communist party expressed a more sharply radical view. The Communist party had in its industrial ranks ex-Wobblies and a large number of foreign-born party members who had emerged out of the Trade Union Unity League (TUUL). The latter, however, remained insulated within their own language group, and although their political rhetoric was revolutionary, they almost never engaged in practical work in relation to other groups.[40] Within the automobile plants their activity was refracted through these language federations. Among such groups as the Armenians, the Rumanians, the Hungarians, and the South Slavs, the Communist party had an influence far beyond its numbers, functioning in may ways as *the* legitimate political organization for a large part of the community. In the Ford plant in Dearborn these groups formed an important constituency for the party, the CIO, and the New Deal—and ultimately for the left wing in the UAW—yet it appears that few men emerged out of these subgroups to play a plant-wide role in the union.[41]

The older, militant cadre of workers proved to be out of touch with American realities. About one-fourth of the TUUL membership resisted the turn to working within the CIO, and these were largely the more insular, foreign-born workers. The native-born TUUL members, whether native Protestant, old immigrant, or the second generation of the new immigrants, were overwhelmingly pro-CIO.[42] And, as George Charney puts it, the impact of the New Deal and the CIO, the twin pillars of mass politics, caused "an internal revolution" in the Communist party.[43] Even before the 1936–1937 political and industrial up-surge, the influx of new members into the Communist party—people who were native-born and essentially liberal-reformist in their perspec-tives—materially altered the character of the party despite the persis-tence of the old-line rhetoric.[44] With the breakthrough in mass produc-tion industries, the influx of this transforming current grew to flood proportions.

The leftist parties had set themselves at the forefront of the organiz-ing drives, emphasizing the day-to-day struggles. "The light we were putting on the Socialist party through our activities [was] that the Socialist party was really another side of the labor movement, that there was a very close relationship between the two—which wasn't exactly true." Kord's assessment is widely applicable. Far from retain-ing their "revolutionary" character while working in the new mass organizations, the new adherents of working-class reformism penetrated and transformed the radical parties. In functioning as the most deter-mined and farseeing exponents of industrial unionism, the radical parties attracted a host of workers on precisely that basis, becoming the nucleus around which the most fervently New Deal and trade-union elements could coalesce. In the bitter faction fight within the UAW, in which the shadow issue of "communism" concealed the real political and ethnocultural divisions within the working class, the Unity Caucus remained the staunchest defender of the New Deal, aggressively com-mitted to the organization of the blacks and the workers of new immigrant background. In this sense it is correct to consider the Left in the CIO an integral part of the New Deal, its organic (rather than antagonistic) left wing. Within the Communist party the rout of the syndicalist Left was consummated at the Cleveland convention of the UAW, at which R. J. Thomas was chosen by the CIO bigwigs who in turn were supported by the Communist party apparatus. While the dispute did not break the surface, appearing only in informal discus-sions off the convention floor, there was a great deal of consternation in Communist and Communist-influenced circles, where it was thought that either Wyndham Mortimer or Ed Hall should have received the presidency.[45]

As we have seen in the present study, the syndicalist Left preferred a more decentralized organizational structure and played down the importance of the contract. At the same time, however, this current was far less political, far less capable of expanding its influence, and was more provincial, less cosmopolitan than the Socialist party group around Kord. Those in the Socialist party group desired to broaden their cultural horizons. Inextricably bound up with their democratic idealism was the desire for education and self-improvement. And, unlike the syndicalists, the Socialists were relatively temperate. This constellation of attitudes and personalities among the political Left on the shop floor seems to have been widespread. The dual themes of collective struggle and self-improvement, of egalitarian ideals and occupational and cultural mobility, were organically intertwined.

In the Detroit automobile industry the Communist party had almost no success among Appalachian migrants and little success among the Poles. Rather, it drew more from among the skilled, from the ranks of those who surrounded the union leadership, from among the more educated, and from among the blacks.[46] And the majority among these men of 1937 and after saw the Communist party as a force in the union for democracy and trade unionism. "A surprisingly large number [of the new members] are union officials. . . . A mere glance at the composition of the people that it is winning proves that beyond doubt . . . its work in the unions, especially in the Committee for Industrial Organization drives, had won to its ranks some of the most active union functionaries and rank and file workers."[47] According to George Charney, of the three to four hundred Communist party members in the Hotel and Restaurant Employees Union in New York 50 percent or more were shop stewards, members of the executive board, delegates, or party bureaucrats.[48] Glazer suggests that when the Communist party failed to control a union, its membership in that union declined. When it controlled a union, its membership rose.[49] Although he puts forth a rather sinister explanation of this, the prosaic truth may be closer to the paradigm that can be constructed out of the experience of Local 229. There were opportunists like Kozik and Watson everywhere; and as the unions grew they were inevitably attracted to whatever power structure seemed to guarantee their advancement. At the Ford Dearborn plant one insider estimates that 25 percent of those who joined

the Communist party after the local was firmly established were opportunists.[50]

Among the blacks a special situation seemed to prevail. Effectively
disenfranchised, without organizational and political structures through
which to assert their interests, they found in the Communist party a
practical means of overcoming these problems.[51] Racism was widespread among the white auto workers, particularly the Appalachian
migrants. In a period when the issue of black advancement was a hot
potato in general, it was even more so in the automobile industry.
Although the Communist party was not the only group to take up the
cause of the black workers, it was the most effective organization to do
so. In a sense, the party picked up where Reconstruction left off,
becoming the focal point for the expression of the repressed bourgeois-
democratic needs of the black workers. These circumstances led to a
situation in which blacks constituted a distinct social and political
group within the Communist party. They tended to be the least
socialist-minded, the most liberal and democratic element in the party.
Because the party fought to promote blacks to leadership positions, the
goal of personal advancement and party membership seemed to merge.
Immediately after the war large numbers of black workers at Ford
enrolled in party schools, preparing themselves for assuming such
lower echelon positions in the union as steward or committeeman.[52]

Although this pattern of trade-union and radical activity took on its
sharpest form in relation to blacks mainly because of the conspicuous
failure of bourgeois society to eradicate caste distinctions, the majority
of native-born white party members, of whatever ethnic background,
were in many ways similar. If the New Deal promised reforms and
advancement through the workings of a vast, impersonal political process, the radical parties gave the more intelligent and aggressive workers
what the Democratic party could not—an education, a cultural experience, and a sense of community that society denied to the mass of
industrial workers.

Nowhere is the social process that underpinned CIO radicalism better
demonstrated than in the experience of the Communist party in recruiting workers in Flint immediately after the war. Workers joined by the
dozens, notes Saul Wellman, state chairman during the postwar years,

not to get deeper into the world of the assembly line but to escape it. For these workers, their imaginations fired by the cultural and intellectual vistas opened up by their experience, life in Flint became intolerable—and they left.[53]

## The Auto Workers: Conservative Tendencies

The integration of the broad mass of the more conservative workers into the union had far-reaching consequences. The victory of the Flint sit-down strike brought a flood of new members into the organization, yet despite the fact that in Flint, for example, it was the Communist and Socialist militants (Bob Travis and two of the Reuther brothers, Victor and Roy) who engineered the victory in the fall of 1937, Homer Martin was easily able to remove them, placing the local under the administrative leadership of Jack Little and reputed Black Legionnaire Bert Harris.[54] In the local elections of February 1938 the Homer Martin slate, headed by Jack Little, easily defeated the Unity slate, heated by Roy Reuther, by a vote of 7,540 to 4,080.[55] In Dodge the weakening of the Left under the impact of the influx of the masses took a few years longer. Until 1942 the Left (largely non-Communist), centered in the trim department, continued to hold the presidency. In that year, however, Mike Novak, a second-generation Pole who had become well known through his work as a leader of the flying squadron (characterized as a political machine by one insider) defeated Earl Reynolds for the presidency.[56] The shift in administration and politics reflected a shift in ethnocultural base. Moreover, the broader involvement of the mass of Polish workers caused the union administration and the Democratic party machine of Hamtramck to become intertwined in the formation of a hybrid political machine, complete with patronage.[57]

The Associated Automobile Workers of America (AAWA) was another conservative pre-CIO independent union that emerged about the same time as the AIWA, splitting off from the AFL federal locals in June 1934. While the AAWA had its main stronghold in the Hudson plant in Detroit, it had significant strength in the General Motors truck plant in Pontiac and the Oldsmobile plant in Lansing, as well as pockets of support in the Plymouth plant in Detroit and the Fisher Body plants in Pontiac and Lansing.[58] How closely this group was allied with company management is, according to Fine, difficult to determine, although the AFL accused the group of being "an outside company union."[59] The individual locals of the AAWA enjoyed "virtually complete autonomy"[60] —certainly a sign of weakness and possibly of company inspiration, but also a sign of a traditional antiparty, antiinstitutional spirit characteristic of Protestant populism.[61] Those areas where the AAWA was strong—Pontiac, Lansing, the Hudson plant—were characterized by a working population that was predominantly native-born, while among the foreign-born British and German backgrounds predominated.[62] Of special significance among the native-born were large numbers of migrants from Appalachia and parts of the South. Therefore the high correlation between areas of AAWA strength and areas of Black Legion activity,[63] and the correlation between these and the strength of the Homer Martin faction are of special importance. Although the area of Homer Martin support was much broader than that of AAWA strength, wherever the latter had been influential in 1934 and 1935 Homer Martin enjoyed significant strength in the NLRB elections of April 17, 1940, Of the combined AFL–Homer Martin and CIO-Unity vote, 33 percent in Pontiac and 35 percent in Lansing went to Homer Martin. Flint, its population characteristics similar to those of Lansing and Pontiac, gave a similarly large percentage of its votes to Homer Martin.[64] The only large local to cast a majority of its votes for Martin was Local 131 in Norwood, Ohio, where three-fourths of the vote went to the AFL and Homer Martin. Ninety-five percent of the workers in Norwood were native-born whites, 50 to 60 percent of them from the hills of Appalachia.[65]

A close examination of the Lansing and Pontiac figures reveals sharp differences. In Lansing, the Fisher Body workers gave Martin only 22 percent of their votes, while the Oldsmobile workers gave him 45 percent. In Pontiac the situation was similar: 22 percent at Fisher Body and 39 percent at Pontiac for Homer Martin. The significance of these figures becomes clearer when we recall that it was in the body plants that both tool-and-die workers and skilled production workers—trimmers, cushion builders, and metal finishers—were concentrated, whereas in the other plants the unskilled assembly work was done. Moreover, in both the Pontiac Motors plant and the Chevrolet plant in Flint, the southern-born were the largest single group of workers.[66] By going back to June 1939 we can get a better idea of the implications of these elections for the future of the union.

Because of the presence of the Homer Martin group in the General Motors plants, the management refused to bargain with the UAW-CIO, claiming that it did not know who really represented the workers. While the CIO was preparing to call a strike, Homer Martin, in anticipation of this strategy, decided to pull a strike in Flint and Saginaw.[67] Before the Martin strike flopped and was called off on June 14, it demonstrated that Martin's greatest strength resided in the final assembly line in the Chevrolet plant in Flint[68] —a department dominated numerically by southern-born workers.[69] On the other hand, the UAW-CIO, weakest among the unskilled production workers in the General Motors empire, restricted its strike call to tool-and-die, maintenance, and other skilled workers in the plants, where it had "its only effective concentration of strength."[70]

With the collapse of the Homer Martin group those elements that had supported Martin ultimately rejoined the CIO (or were brought under the jurisdiction of the CIO), but by no means did they lose their distinctive historical characteristics. The expansion and consolidation of the UAW following the tool-and-die strike against General Motors in June of 1939 and the NLRB elections of early 1940 involved the assimilation of a vast mass of workers radically dissimilar from those who had originally built the union. Both the anti-CIO rural Protestants and the pro-CIO new immigrants would necessarily have their impact on the political structure of the union. Whatever the wishes of the leadership, a transformation was inevitable.

An obscure but important indication of working-class conservatism is found in the role of fraternal organizations not of the foreign-born, but of the native-born. Influential networks of Masons and Knights of Columbus permeated most if not all of the plants (we saw the Masons in action in Local 229), representing two of the more conservative groups of northern-born white workers—the WASPs and the old-stock Catholics, respectively. These networks included numerous foremen, some higher management people, and many workers (probably weighted toward the skilled end of the occupational spectrum). In-periods of unemployment, particularly, Masons would be given prefer-ence over others. The solidarity of the Masons in the Detroit Parts Company has already been noted; in other plants a similar situation existed.[71] The influence of the Masons was sufficiently pervasive to emerge as a kind of caucus at the 1936 UAW convention, where it got Walter N. Wells elected third vice-president.[72] In the 1950s a Mason succeeded in becoming elected president of the Buick local in Flint solely on the basis of his membership in the fraternal order.[73]

We can only speculate at this point as to the significance of the Masons (more information has surfaced about them than about the Knights of Columbus). It seems clear that the WASP ethnocultural milieu and concept of community could sustain its separate identity on a fairly high organizational level—whether in the form of a faction in the UAW, as in the case of the Masonic caucus that got Wells elected third vice-president, or in the form of an anti-union association, as with the case of Al Schein in Local 229. The only instance which has come to my attention so far of a local union's being taken over by a Masonic faction—that of Buick in Flint—provides some basis for informed specu-lation. The work force at Buick was drawn largely from the commu-nity, the pattern of hiring followed the lines of family relationships, and the men in management were generally promoted from the ranks of the workers.[74] It was the kind of stable, face-to-face, and somewhat archaic system of relationships that was unheard of in the Fisher Body plants. It appears that the Masons may have had their greatest influence where the older Anglo-Saxon community persisted, where modern bureaucratic rationality had as yet failed to penetrate very deeply, and where the plant "community" itself was fairly stable and ethnically homogeneous.

The drollest story of the influence of a working-class subculture involves the Yellow Cab Plant in Pontiac, soon after the UAW-CIO was reconstituted there in 1939. At that time there existed a network of barroom cliques, at the center of which was Charlie X. In 1939 X decided to make a run for the presidency of the local, on the basis of no program whatsoever, and without giving a shred of evidence that he could handle even the rudiments of the job. His opponent, the incumbent Cliff Williams, a capable, experienced, and courageous unionist, bore a good deal of the responsibility for the ultimate success of the CIO in Pontiac. Yet it soon became apparent to Williams that X had a good chance of winning, for the network of barroom cliques embraced almost half the workers of the plant, and there was no doubt that X would garner virtually all the votes of his buddies and admirers. What followed was a remarkable burlesque. Williams convinced X to make a deal. Williams would support X for president, and X would support Williams for vice-president, with the written understanding that X would resign after thirty days. The election went off as planned, but when the thirty days were up X decided to remain as president. Despite his promise, of which he was reminded, X refused to budge. Finally, Williams and his group invited X to a hotel suite where they wined him and dined him, but most particularly wined him (on a fifth of whiskey and a case of beer) until he got extremely drunk, whereupon they got him to sign a statement which they then had notarized. The upshot: Williams stepped into the vacated presidency as planned, if a little bit late. [75]

Expansion of the union was thus a two-edged sword. If in theory the Left welcomed the chance to draw in the broad mass of workers, in practice the working class was not so much influenced by the Left as the UAW was influenced by the church, the political machine, several kinds of rural Protestant conservatism, and a variety of local prepolitical subcultures. In the last analysis, the political and institutional development of the union bears witness to the historical character of the broad masses of workers who were brought within its framework. The process of bureaucratization was a consequence, not of the "motives" of the bureaucrats, but rather of the complex structure of the situation itself.

**NOTES**

**INDEX**

# Notes

## Introduction: Theory, Method, and Oral History

1. This evidence includes Constance S. Tonat, "A Case Study of a Local Union: Participation, Loyalty and Attitudes of Local Union Members" (M.A. thesis, Wayne State University, Detroit, 1956), which is based on a study of Local 229; a few brief notices which appeared in the *United Automobile Worker* between 1938 and 1940; and a collection of correspondence found in the George F. Addes Papers on deposit at the Archives of Labor History and Urban Affairs at Wayne State University (henceforth cited as Archives).

2. The material contained in the Archives pertaining to Local 229 is sparse. Even in regard to two of the most thoroughly documented locals—Local 51 (Plymouth) and Local 3 (Dodge)—the materials available are of such character as to render impossible any attempt at answering the questions posed in the present study.

3. This problem is taken up in chapter 8.

4. The *East European Quarterly*, 3 (January 1970) is devoted to a symposium entitled "Peasantry and Industrialization in Eastern Europe."

5. Sidney Fine, *The Automobile Under the Blue Eagle* (Ann Arbor: University of Michigan Press, 1963); Sidney Fine, *Sit-down: The General Motors Strike of 1936–1937* (Ann Arbor: University of Michigan Press, 1969). These books proved to be invaluable references. The wealth of detail in *The Automobile Under the Blue Eagle* is staggering.

6. Fine, *The Automobile Under the Blue Eagle*, p. 149.

7. Ibid.

8. Fine, *Sit-down*, p. 98.

9. Ibid.

10. Paul Kleppner, *The Cross of Culture: A Social Analysis of Midwestern Politics, 1880–1900* (New York: Free Press, 1970); and Frederick C. Luebke, *Immigrants and Politics: The Germans of Nebraska, 1880–1900* (Lincoln: University of Nebraska Press, 1969).

11. Nancy S. Struever, "The Study of Language and the Study of History," *The Journal of Interdisciplinary History*, 4 (Winter 1974): 411.

12. See Martin Jay, *The Dialectical Imagination: A History of the Frankfurt School and the Institute of Social Research, 1923–1950* (Boston: Little, Brown, 1973), pp. 43–53. "So-called *objective* historiography had just consisted in treating historical conditions as separate from activity. Reactionary character." Addendum in Marx's handwriting in the manuscript of *The German Ideology* in Loyd D. Easton and Kurt H. Guddat, *Writings of the Young Marx on Philosophy and Society* (Garden City, N.Y.: Doubleday, 1967), p. 433.

13. The problem of language as practice in this sense is one of the central points of Ludwig Wittgenstein, *Philosophical Investigations* (Oxford: Basil Blackwell, 1963).

14. On the Hegelian-Marxist critique of positivism, see Jurgen Habermas, *Knowledge and Human Interests* (Boston: Beacon Press, 1968); George Lukacs, "What is Orthodox Marxism?" in *History and Class Consciousness: Studies in Marxist Dialectics* (Cambridge, Mass.: MIT Press, 1968); Max Horkheimer, "Traditional and Critical Theory," in *Critical Theory: Selected Essays* (New York: Herder and Herder, 1972); The Frankfurt Institute for Social Research, *Aspects of Sociology* (Boston: Beacon Press, 1972); and Jay, *The Dialectical Imagination*, especially pp. 54–60, 82. On the historical situatedness of the historian and the problem of the *intentionality* of historical thought, see Ludwig Landgrebe, *Major Problems in Contemporary European Philosophy from Dilthey to Heidegger* (New York: F. Ungar, 1966). Also see Louis Althusser and Etienne Balibar, *Reading Capital* (London: NLB, 1970), chaps. 4 and 5.

History, as it is practiced today, does not turn its back on events; on the contrary, it is continually enlarging the field of events, constantly discovering new layers—more superficial as well as more profound—incessantly isolating new ensembles—events, numerous, dense and interchangeable or rare and decisive: from daily price fluctuations to secular inflations. What is significant is that history does not consider an event without defining the series to which it belongs, without specifying the method of analysis used, without seeking the regularity of phenomena and the probable limits of their occurrence. . . . History has long since abandoned its attempts to understand events in terms of cause and effect. . . . It did not do this in order to seek out structures alien or hostile to the event. It was rather in order to establish those diverse converging, and sometimes divergent, but never autonomous series that enables us to circumscribe the "locus" of an event, the limits to its fluidity and the conditions of its emergence. [Michel Foucault, *The Archaeology of Knowledge* (New York: Pantheon Books, 1972), p. 230.]

15. Clifford Geertz, *The Interpretation of Cultures* (New York: Basic Books, 1973), p. 14.

16. Ibid., pp. 25–26.

17. Ibid., p. 15.

18. Jean Piaget, *Structuralism* (New York: Harper and Row, 1971).

19. John G. Kruchko, *The Birth of a Union Local: The History of UAW Local 674, Norwood, Ohio, 1933–1940* (Ithaca, N. Y.: New York State School of Industrial and Labor Relations, Cornell University, 1972), p. iii.

20. The following is an example of the generation of data. The excerpts are from my interview with Frank Fagan of August 9, 1974. Fagan was active in Murray Body during the formative years of the UAW.

FAGAN: In Murray there was a predominance of Polish people. And I always had the feeling that they—although I don't know this to be a fact—they're all pretty close. Nearly all lived in Hamtramck, which was near by.... There seemed to be a predominance of Polish—I realized that when I first got active in the union when we actually got recognized and I had to keep book as a steward.

FRIEDLANDER: Steward in the welding department?

FAGAN: Well, the body in white. I covered quite a large building. I'm talking now about after we organized the union ... later 1937, late '36. I know I had a predominance of Polish there, because I had trouble with the names ...

FRIEDLANDER:When you shouldered union responsibilities and you were going around and checking up on people, how widely did you travel in body in white?

FAGAN: The whole thing.

FRIEDLANDER: I assume you know that best then?

FAGAN: Yeah....

FRIEDLANDER: I find that there's a lot of Hungarians floating around metal-finishing. Now is that true here?

FAGAN: I, I don't ... I'm sitting here thinking about the metal-finishing gang, all the guys on the different floors that I knew. I don't recall a metal finisher that wasn't a great big strong Polish fella in Murray Body.

FRIEDLANDER: So they're all Polish in Murray Body?

FAGAN: Yeah. Come to think of it.... I'm just thinking about all the lists of names of the metal finishers, because I used to list them for wage negotiations, always trying to get them up higher.

FRIEDLANDER: I just want to double-check something. There's no chance of your confusing a Polish name with some other Slavic nationality?

FAGAN: There's that possibility, but not very great possibility. I knew everyone.

FRIEDLANDER: Between Yugoslav on the one hand, and Rumanian and Hungarian on the other hand ...

FAGAN: No, I don't think I could have made that mistake. There might have been some, but I doubt it very much. It just seems to me they were nearly all Polish. Even the foremen.... I don't think—I can't recall any one that I don't know—because we had a lot of affairs going where we needed their names and that sort of thing.

21. Interview with Frank Fagan, February 19, 1963, Archives, pp. 10–11.

## Chapter 1: In the Beginning

1. Arthur Evans Wood, *Hamtramck: A Sociological Study of a Polish-American Community* (New Haven: College and University Press, 1962), p. 46.

2. Ibid., p. 29; interview with Stanley Nowak, February 26, 1974, Detroit.

3. Nowak interview.

4. Wood, *Hamtramck*, p. 30; Nowak interview.

5. Nowak interview; Edmund Kord interviews; interview with Bernard Wnuk, October 22, 1973, Binghamton, N. Y.

6. See William I. Thomas and Florian Znaniecki, *The Polish Peasant in Europe and America* (New York: Dover Publications, 1958), pp. 98–112, 706–11.

7. Father Coughlin, famed radio priest of Detroit in the 1930s, espoused a populist anti-Communist program, denouncing international bankers, and urging government intervention to protect workers from exploitation. His radio program had an immense following made up mainly of old-stock (Irish and German) Catholics and German Lutherans. After flirting briefly with a number of independent unions in the early thirties, Coughlin came out in opposition to the fledgling UAW, which he denounced as Communist-led. See Seymour Martin Lipset and Earl Raab, *The Politics of Unreason: Right-Wing Extremism in America, 1790– 1970* (New York: Harper and Row, 1970), pp. 167–89; Charles J. Tull, *Father Coughlin and the New Deal* (Syracuse: Syracuse University Press, 1965), p. 174.

8. Margaret Collingwood Nowak, "The Making of an American: The Story of Stanley Nowak," undated manuscript, p. 153, Stanley Nowak Collection, Archives of Labor History and Urban Affairs, Wayne State University (henceforth cited as Archives).

9. Ibid.

10. Sidney Fine, *The Automobile Under the Blue Eagle* (Ann Arbor: University of Michigan Press, 1963), pp. 26–27, 42, 63–71.

11. Quoted in Sidney Fine, *Sit-down: The General Motors Strike of 1936– 1937* (Ann Arbor: University of Michigan Press, 1969), p. 96.

12. John M. Allswang, *A House for All Peoples: Ethnic Politics in Chicago, 1890–1936* (Lexington: University Press of Kentucky, 1971), p. 12; Edgar Eugene Robinson, *They Voted for Roosevelt: The Presidential Vote, 1932–1944* (Stanford, Calif.: Stanford University Press, 1947).

13. Wood, *Hamtramck*, p. 101.

14. Fine, *Sit-down*, pp. 128–33.

15. Ibid., pp. 222, 223–24. 311; Jerold S. Auerbach, *Labor and Liberty: The La Follette Committee and the New Deal* (Indianapolis: Bobbs-Merrill, 1966); George F. Addes, secretary-treasurer of the UAW, to all officers and members of local unions, December 15, 1936, in the Richard T. Frankensteen Collection, box 1, Archives.

16. Wood, *Hamtramck*, pp. 76–77; John A. Zaremba, recording secretary of Local 3, to the members of Dodge Local 3 in regard to April 1940 Hamtramck municipal elections, March 25, 1940; Zaremba to Walter Kanar, mayor of Ham-

tramck, March 25, 1940. Both letters are in the Frankensteen Collection, box 1, Archives.

17. Frankensteen Collection, box 1, Archives.

18. Wood, *Hamtramck*, pp. 59–64, 68–70.

19. *United Automobile Worker*, Dodge Local 3 edition, September 1, 1936; *New York Times*, March 18, 1937.

20. *United Automobile Worker*, Dodge Local 3 edition, September 1, 1936; Nowak, "The Making of an American," pp. 254–77.

21. Kord is not certain that Jaskiewicz and Zyznomyrsky were at the first meeting, although he considers it likely—more so in regard to Jaskiewicz. There is enough circumstantial evidence to suggest strongly that they were. There were others at the first meeting besides those from torch- and front-welding, and Jaskiewicz and Zyznomyrsky were the two best secondary leaders in the shop at that time. Kord is sure that they attended the second meeting and that they had in fact become active before that time. It is also likely that George Kiertanis, a second-generation Lithuanian press operator in department 19, had joined by this time. Kiertanis played a role on the day shift similar to that played by Johnny Zyznomyrsky on the afternoon shift, although he was probably less active than Zyznomyrsky.

22. J. Woodford Howard, Jr., *Mr. Justice Murphy: A Political Biography* (Princeton, N.J.: Princeton University Press, 1968), p. 150.

23. Ibid., p. 147.

24. *Newsweek* (March 6, 1937, pp. 8–10) gives a vivid if prejudiced account of Chrysler's discomfort in the union-run city.

## Chapter 2: Early Confrontations

1. Sidney Fine, *Sit-down: The General Motors Strike of 1936–1937* (Ann Arbor: University of Michigan Press, 1969), pp. 327–28.

2. Interview with Richard T. Frankensteen, October 10, 23, 1959; November 6, 1959; December 7, 1961, pp. 28–29, Archives of Labor History and Urban Affairs, Wayne State University.

## Chapter 3: Offensive

1. The exceptions that Kord recalls were Nick Buglaj, the first-generation Ukrainian in swaging; Johnny Galinsky, who we recall was the last holdout in torch-welding and who was brought into the union under peer pressure; John Novak, the Slovak Communist in the toolroom; and "Russian John," an American-born press operator who grew up in Russia, became influenced by the Russian Revolution, and later returned to the United States. He was a militant, though somewhat isolated because he spoke only broken English and thus could not become a leader among the second generation.

2. The two exceptions that Kord recalls were William Cooper, who of the Appalachian migrants had resided in the north the longest and was most at ease among the second-generation workers, and Hillbilly, the last holdout in torch-welding with the exception of Johnny Galinsky. Like Galinsky, Hillbilly had been brought into the union under peer pressure.

3. "In a community so heavily weighted with foreign-born labor, the workers' frame of mind resembles the ancient continental attitude of peasant to landlord; envy, distrust, and adoration; veneration mixed with contempt; fear coupled with hatred; all diluted by the stoic indifference which is induced by the more or less successful efforts to gain one's daily bread and rear one's family in peace" (Philip Klein, *A Social Study of Pittsburgh: Community Problems and Social Services in Allegheny County* [New York: Columbia University Press, 1938], p. 302).

Is it possible that other, more pragmatic and secular considerations were responsible for this attitude on the part of the first-generation Poles? As far as Kord is aware, these immigrant workers had not been involved in the tragic defeats of the earlier period of labor upheaval, the high point of which was the Great Steel Strike of 1919.

4. In retrospect, this view seems unduly pessimistic.

5. Classification seniority within a department worked as follows: in torch-welding, for example, the classifications were those of grinder, helper, and welder. Under classification seniority a worker could not move from one class to another, or from one department to another within the same class. One of the effects of this form of seniority was that it more or less prevented advancement within the plant for the unskilled workers. Another effect was that it tended to fragment the workers into competing interest groups. As is seen in chapter 5, the conflict that developed over seniority was both bitter and dangerous.

## Chapter 5: Factionalism

1. Minutes of the Chrysler Conference, January 28, 1938, box 1, George F. Addes Papers, Archives of Labor History and Urban Affairs, Wayne State University.

2. These wildcat actions began to taper off after 1938. See Constance S. Tonat, "A Case Study of a Local Union: Participation, Loyalty and Attitudes of Local Union Members" (M.A. thesis, Wayne State University, Detroit, 1956), p. 23.

## Chapter 6: Consolidation

1. *Detroit News*, April 4, 16, 17, 18, 19, and 21, 1938.

2. *United Automobile Worker*, November 1938. To forestall discovery of the identity of the local the exact date is not given.

3. In Region 1 this percentage was much higher. Of the forty-four contracts negotiated in this region between August 1, 1939, and January 31, 1940, twenty included vacations with pay. See Six Months' Report of Activities and Expendition, Archives of Labor History and Urban Affairs, Wayne State University.

## Chapter 7: Culture and Structure

1. Stanley Kicinski, a first-generation Pole whose mechanical ability made him almost unique among those of his background, and whose English, though broken, was much better than that of the other first-generation workers, later joined Buglaj as the only other first-generation steward.

2. See also interview with Frank Marquart, February 10 and 24, 1960, and September 5, 1961, Archives of Labor History and Urban Affairs, Wayne State University. Marquart's account of the Socialist party in Detroit is virtually identical to Kord's.

## Chapter 8: Conclusion: The Union and the Outside World

1. Sidney Fine, *Sit-down: The General Motors Strike of 1936–1937* (Ann Arbor: University of Michigan Press, 1969); Sidney Fine, *The Automobile Under the Blue Eagle* (Ann Arbor: University of Michigan Press, 1963); Irving Bernstein, *Turbulent Years: A History of the American Worker, 1933–1941* (Boston: Houghton Mifflin, 1971); Theodore V. Purcell, *Blue Collar Man: Patterns of Dual Allegiance in Industry* (Cambridge, Mass.: Harvard University Press, 1960); Theodore V. Purcell, *The Worker Speaks His Mind on Company and Union* (Cambridge, Mass.: Harvard University Press, 1953); Jeremy Brecher, *Strike!* (San Francisco: Straight Arrow Books, 1972); Stanley Aronowitz, *False Promises: The Shaping of American Working Class Consciousness* (New York: McGraw-Hill, 1973). I use the term *syndicalist* rather loosely to cover the emphasis of the latter two authors on spontaneous working-class activity, and their hostility toward institutions.

2. Leon Trotsky, *Writings of Leon Trotsky, 1939–1940*, ed. George Breitman and Evelyn Reed (New York: Pathfinder Press, 1969), p. 61.

3. Ibid., p. 62.

4. Factionalism in the UAW was quite involved. Basically, there were two periods of major factional conflicts. The struggle between the Homer Martin forces known as the Progressives (themselves a coalition of heterogeneous elements) and the Unity Forces (which included a number of influential and powerful Communists and Socialists) erupted into the open in the spring of 1937 and led to the splitting of the union in March 1939. The issue of communism raised by the Martin forces appealed to the nativist and antiforeign elements in

the union, although the structure of the Martin group was more complex than that. With the Martin forces vanquished, the Unity Caucus began to come apart, with Socialists on one side (and beginning to pick up the support of the Association of Catholic Trade Unionists) and Communists on the other. It should be noted, however, that the Communists were a minority in this so-called Left caucus (Addes, Thomas, and Frankensteen). If the Ford local can be the basis for some tentative inferences, the Left appeared to have the support of the South Slavs, the Hungarians, the Rumanians, the blacks, and the British and North European tool-and-die makers, while the Right (the Reuther forces) appeared to have the support of the Catholics, especially the second generation among the East Europeans, the older-stock Catholics, and probably fragments of others. The struggle between the two factions came to a climax in the immediate postwar years, when the Left was defeated at the UAW conventions and many of its pro-Communist members driven from positions of influence.

5. For an idea of the structure and concerns of the region, see Richard T. Frankensteen and Leo LaMotte, Region No. 1 Report (for the period April through June 1939), George F. Addes Collection, box 1, Archives of Labor History and Urban Affairs, Wayne State University (henceforth cited as Archives); and Six Months' Report of Activities and Expenditures, Region 1–UAW-CIO (for the period August 1, 1939, through January 31, 1940), John A. Zaremba Collection, box 9, Archives.

6. Fine, *The Automobile Under the Blue Eagle*, pp. 337–41.

7. Interview with Richard Harris, November 16, 1959, Archives.

8. Leaflet entitled "Automotive Industrial Workers Association Members: We Swept the Primary Election for the Union!" in the Henry Kraus Collection, box 16, Archives; and Minutes of the First Annual Convention of Delegates of the Automobile Industrial Workers Association, October 12, 13, 1935, Zaremba Collection, box 6, Archives.

9. Speech in Richard T. Frankensteen Collection, box 1, Archives. Frankensteen, speaking of the situation in New England, refers to the "honest Puritan stock [who] worked faithfully," and to the manufacturers who denied their humble requests for a living wage and "arbitrarily sent to Southern Europe for illiterate, ignorant peasants to replace the good old Puritan stock. Within two years Communism was born and from then on no requests were made but they were demands with alternatives–alternatives that brought on a flow of strikes of sabotage and of murders." He then goes on to ask the employers to recognize the rights of workers under Constitutional law to organize and expressed hope that "you will deal with them as honest men and gentlemen that they are and not create a new class of Communists and crooks." The last two words were crossed out.

10. Seymour Martin Lipset and Earl Raab, *The Politics of Unreason: Right-Wing Extremism in America, 1790–1970* (New York: Harper and Row, 1970), pp. 167–78.

11. Roll Call of Shop Stewards, Zaremba Collection, box 9, Archives; UAW Dodge Local #3 Results of the Election for Delegates to UAW-CIO Convention at St. Louis, Mo., personal collection of Joe Adams; List of Delegates to CIO Convention, Zaremba Collection, box 9, Archives; Dodge Organizing Committee, List of Committee Members, Trustees, Executive Board Members, Plant Committee, and Dodge Organizing Committee, Zaremba Collection, box 9, Archives; interview with Earl Reynolds, January 12, 1974, Detroit; interview with Joe Adams, February 27, March 1, and March 5, 1974, Detroit.

12. An undated leaflet in the Frankensteen Collection, box 1, Archives, contains the following statement: "The Cushion Line at Dodge Brothers are proud of the fact that the night group have all but two men organized." Adams and Reynolds interviews.

13. Interview with Richard T. Frankensteen, October 10, 23, 1959; November 6, 1959; December 7, 1961, Archives.

14. Harris interview.

15. Local 3, Minutes of Executive Board Meeting, May 20, 1937, Archives. Note the motion by Brother Seymour: "In view of the fact that the vote cast was under 10,000, therefore when publishing election results on bulletin boards, the amount of votes be eliminated and only the winners should be posted, without stating what amount of votes elected each man."

16. *Detroit News*, February 18, 1938; Wyndham Mortimer to CIO Director John Brophy, March 20, 1938, Kraus Collection, box 13, Archives.

17. Inasmuch as an exact citation would reveal the identity of the local, the citation is omitted.

18. Citation omitted for the same reason as above.

19. Addressee omitted to prevent identification of local.

20. Frank Fagan's account of the selection and character of the delegates to the UAW conventions as well as his description of the levels of political understanding in the Murray Body local are in essence very similar to the situation in the Detroit Parts local. Interview with Frank Fagan, August 9, 12, 20, 1974, Detroit.

21. Interview with Everett Francis, October 13, 20, 27, 1961, Archives; interview with Bud Simons, September 6, 1960, Archives.

22. Interview with John W. Anderson, December 22, 1973, Dearborn; interview with Leon Pody, November 28, 1959, January 11, 1960, Archives; Fine, *The Automobile Under the Blue Eagle*, p. 176.

23. Interview with Al Rightly, January 11, 1974, Detroit.

24. Pody, Reynolds, and Adams interviews; AIWA Dues Book, Frankensteen Collection, box 1, Archives.

25. Pody interview; interview with Adam Poplewski, May 2, 1960, Archives; interview with John K. McDaniel, May 26, 1961, Archives; Anderson interview (on role of metal finishers throughout Detroit).

26. Anderson and Adams interviews. "Trimming was one of the semi-skilled production jobs along with a few others in the automobile industry such as

painting, metal-finishing, soldering and welding" (Francis interview). "Metal finishing was regarded as a skilled trade" (Poplewski interview).

27. Rightly and Anderson interviews.

28. Interview with Paul Russo, April 13, 1961, Archives.

29. Pody interview.

30. Simons interview.

31. Interview with Harry Ross, July 10, 1961, Archives.

32. McDaniel interview.

33. Frankensteen interview.

34. Harris interview.

35. Interview with Tracy Doll, April 21, 1961, Archives.

36. Interview with Edgar Lock, January 10, 1974, Detroit.

37. Interview with George Charney, May 15, 1973, New York.

38. Rebecca Grecht, "Let Us Keep Our New Members," *Party Organizer*, January 1938.

39. Trotsky, *Writings* p. 64.

40. See Nathan Glazer, *The Social Basis of American Communism* (New York: Harcourt, Brace, 1961), pp. 98–99, for a description of the predominance of fraternal over industrial activities in the language groups. George Charney has noted that the predominantly working-class members of a Swedish language fraternal (temperance) organization sympathetic to the Communist party were uninterested in union activities, despite efforts to get them involved. Charney interview, May 9, 1973, New York.

41. Lock interview; interview with Percy Llewelyn, January 12, 1974, Dearborn.

42. Charney interview, May 9, 1973.

43. George Charney, *A Long Journey* (Chicago: Quadrangle Books, 1968), pp. 73–74.

44. In this period the old-timers still placed great emphasis on rhetoric, but the new members had a different implicit orientation. For example, at the Thirteenth Plenum LaGuardia was seen as the main enemy, but "many of us felt bad that we couldn't support LaGuardia." Thus, the move toward the Popular Front policies was developed spontaneously among the newer members of the party. Charney interview, May 9, 1973.

45. Wyndham Mortimer, *Organize! My Life as a Union Man* (Boston: Beacon Press, 1971), pp. 162–64.

46. Charney interview, May 15, 1973.

47. George Morris, "Successful Recruiting Campaign of the C.P.U.S.A.," *International Press Conference*, February 19, 1938, p. 139, quoted in Glazer, *The Social Basis of American Communism*, pp. 115–16.

48. Charney interview, May 15, 1973.

49. Glazer, *The Social Basis of American Communism*, p. 115.

50. It was thought best to omit explicit reference to the source of the estimate.

51. A similar situation obtained in New York City, where the Communist party had perhaps thirty or forty members in the predominantly Italian East Harlem, in contrast to the approximately one thousand members that it had in the much smaller Puerto Rican community. The suggestion is that in the absence in the Puerto Rican community of the strong political organization of Vito Marcantonio (which he inherited from Fiorello LaGuardia) the Communist party filled an organizational vacuum. Charney interview, May 9, 1973.

52. Lock interview; Charney interview, May 15, 1973; interview with Saul Wellman, January 3, 1974, Detroit; Reynolds interview.

53. Wellman interview.

54. Robert Travis, Report on Flint, Kraus Collection, box 12, Archives; Mortimer to Brophy, September 29, 1937, Kraus Collection, box 12, Archives; Mortimer, *Organize!*, pp. 153–54. The Black Legion was a secret society formed by former Klansmen in the industrial cities in Indiana, Ohio, and Michigan. Its members were largely unskilled and semiskilled workers who had migrated to the industrial areas from the hill sections of the South. See Lipset and Raab, *The Politics of Unreason*, pp. 157–59.

55. *Detroit News*, February 18, 1938.

56. Reynolds Interview.

57. See John A. Zaremba to Walter Kanar, mayor of Hamtramck, March 25, 1940, Frankensteen Collection, box 1, Archives. The letter deserves to be quoted in full.

> Dear Sir:
>
> I the undersigned, have been approached by the members of the Heat Treat Core Assembly and Foundry Unit, same unit being a part of Dodge Local #3, that I appeal to your person on behalf of Mr. Alec ____, 2432 ____ St., Hamtramck, Mich., who is an applicant for the position of a Fireman. From the information that I have received, it was understood that two such positions would be filled with members of the Ukrainian nationality, and I have been given assurance that the St. Mary's Parish and the Hamtramck Democratic Political Club have given endorsements for that position to Mr. ____. The members of the Unit mentioned who also as members of Dodge Local #3, kindly request that you give your kind consideration to Mr. ____ for the position mentioned above. Thanking you and I beg to remain
>
> > Respectfully yours
> > John A. Zaremba, Rec. Sec.
> > Dodge Local #3

58. Fine, *The Automobile Under the Blue Eagle*, p. 299 and note 23, p. 500.

59. Ibid., p. 299; "Statement of AFL Rank and File Committee on the Secession of the Hudson Local (Greer) and Other Locals from the American Federation of Labor . . . ," Kraus Collection, box 4, Archives.

60. Fine, *The Automobile Under the Blue Eagle*, p. 299.

61. See Ronald P. Formisano, *The Birth of Mass Political Parties: Michigan, 1827–1861* (Princeton, N. J.: Princeton University Press, 1971), pp. 58–80.

62. U.S., Department of Commerce, Bureau of the Census, *Fifteenth Census of the United States: 1930, Population*, vol. III, tables 18 and 19.

63. Maurice Sugar, memo on the Black Legion, Kraus Collection, box 7, Archives. This memo links the AAWA with the Black Legion, noting that Tyce Woody, president of the Pontiac local of the AAWA, had joined the latter organization. A number of Black Legion members had become leaders in the local unions, according to Sugar. See also *Report of Black Legion Activities in Oakland County* (issued in 1936), George P. Hartrick, Circuit Court Judge presiding, in folder titled "Black Legion," Joe Brown Collection, Archives; and Elmer Akers, "A Social-Psychological Interpretation of the Black Legion," in folder titled "Black Legion," Brown Collection, Archives.

64. *United Automobile Worker*, April 24, 1940.

65. John G. Kruchko, *The Birth of a Union Local: The History of UAW Local 674, Norwood, Ohio, 1933–1940* (Ithaca, N.Y.: New York State School of Industrial and Labor Relations, Cornell University, 1972), pp. 13, 61–62.

66. Interview with Norman Bully, August 8, 1974; interview with Clifton Williams, August 16, 1974, Pontiac; interview with Clifton Williams and Burt Henson, August 21, 1974, Pontiac.

67. Clayton W. Fountain, *Union Guy* (New York: Viking Press, 1949), pp. 107–08.

68. *Detroit Free Press*, June 10, 1939.

69. Not all southern-born workers were Homer Martin supporters. Among the southern-born workers in Pontiac, Michigan, the move from assembly (the least skilled of production jobs) to machine operator was part of a broader process of social and individual development. The new entrants into the industrial work force began as assemblers, retained their ties to the stem family, returned to their homes in the South during seasonal layoffs, and tended to support the Homer Martin forces in the union—although they were generally not organizationally responsive, regardless of faction. (A lot of Homer Martin leadership was drawn from native Catholic elements who were anti-Communist, but from a somewhat different perspective than the southern born.) The workers who became machine operators, however, tended to be those who had been in the northern part of the country longer, and who had severed their ties with the South to a greater extent. Furthermore, it seems that of those southern-born workers who supported the CIO, a large number of them came from this group of occupationally mobile, acculturated urban workers. (One thinks of William Cooper in the front-welding department of the Detroit Parts Company.) Their evangelical commitment to the UAW was for them a commitment to an urban way of life as much as it was to trade unionism. The culture of the uprooted southern migrant was particularly ill-adapted to the industrial environment, and therefore for those who made the

transition, the union played a large role in social and cultural existence. Williams interviews.

70. This may nevertheless be an overstatement. Frederick H. Harbison and Robert Dubin, *Patterns of Union-Management Relations* (Chicago: Science Research Associates, 1947), p. 22; *New Republic*, August 10, 1938, p. 7.

71. Fagan interview.

72. Interview with Carl Haessler, November 27, 1969, and October 24, 1960, Archives.

73. Bully interview.

74. Ibid.

75. Williams interviews.

# Index